THE VILLAGE

AN ORAL HISTORICAL AND ETHNOGRAPHIC STUDY OF A BLACK COMMUNITY

By Wilbur H. Watson

Cleveland   Atlanta   New York

VILLAGE VANGUARD, INC.
Atlanta, Georgia 30314

Library of Congress Cataloging in Publication Data

Main entry under title:

Watson, Wilbur H.

THE VILLAGE: AN ORAL HISTORICAL AND ETHNOGRAPHIC STUDY OF A BLACK COMMUNITY

Contents: Autobiography/ Social History/ Family/ Religion/ Economics of Development/ Sociology of Knowledge and History/ Community/ Black Studies/ Oral Historical Method

1. Afro-American Studies. 2. Community Studies - United States. 3. Sociology of Knowledge and History - United States. 4. Oral Historical and Ethnographic Methods.

ISBN 0-9621460-0-5

(C) 1989 by Village Vanguard, Inc., P. O. Box 42643, Atlanta, Georgia, 30311-0643

All rights reserved. No part of this book may be reproduced in any form or by any means without permission in writing from the publisher.

Printed in the United States.

```
977.1 W343v
Watson, Wilbur H.
The village
```

THE VILLAGE

AN ORAL HISTORICAL AND ETHNOGRAPHIC STUDY OF A BLACK COMMUNITY

DEDICATION

To the memory of my great uncle, Alvin Dark (father's father's brother)

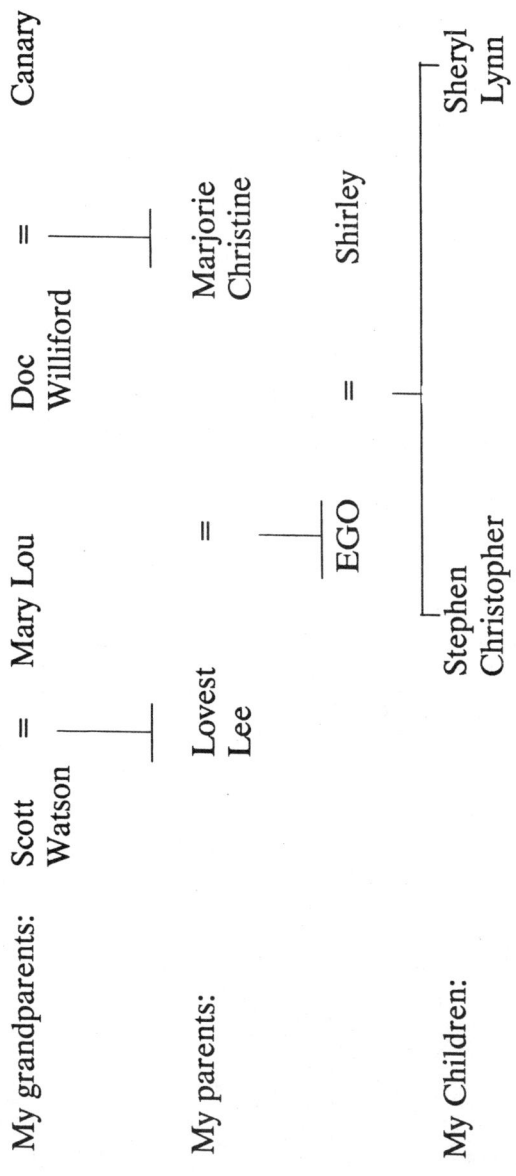

TABLE OF CONTENTS

	Page
Foreword By James E. Blackwell	vii
Preface	xv

CHAPTERS

1. Interfaces of Autobiography and Social History	1
2. Everybody Was Family	12
3. Power and Politics	44
4. Health, Illness and Coping With Adversity	66
5. Wade in the Water	80
6. Private Enterprise and Economics of Development	106
7. Summary and Conclusions	124
8. Afterword: On the Social Construction of Social History	133
Appendix: Key Libraries, Archives and Oral Historians For This Study	153
Endnotes	157
References	189
Subject Index	200

FOREWORD

From the pioneer works of Ferdinand Tonnies and Emile Durkheim to Wilbur Watson's study of THE VILLAGE, a number of informative and sociologically useful interpretations of community life have appeared. Tonnies[1] used the concepts *gemeinschaft* and *gesellschaft* to differentiate between the relatively simple, cohesive social units found in villages, peasant societies, and small towns and the more complex, formalized, transient social structures which characterize urban systems. Durkheim[2] referred to the social units that Tonnies called a *gemeinschaft* by the term "mechanical solidarity"; for him, *gesellschaft* became a system aptly labeled "organic solidarity."

In a *gemeinschaft*, social units are organized on the basis of shared values, easily identified and acceptable social norms, a sense of belonging or a "we" feeling, as it were, loyalty to the group, concern for the welfare of the group as a social enterprise as well as for the general welfare of other members of the social unit or community. Roles in a *gemeinschaft* are unambiguous, and members of the community seem proud of established traditions and patterns of social interaction. In that sense, the social structure and the behavior of members of the component social units assume somewhat mechanical attributes. By contrast, in a *gesellschaft*, a term that usually characterizes the more complex urban societies, there is less consensus around roles, norms and values; there is a high degree of role ambiguity and role conflict; commitment to the group generally is weaker since individuals are more often than not motivated by selfish interests and easily influenced by the changing patterns of social relationships generated frequently by demographic shifts and transformations within urban social systems.

Other community paradigms have concentrated on attachments between individuals and constituent groups,[3] the power structure within groups that result in an elite group having hegemony over the decision-making processes or on pluralistic units depicted as a whole,[4] or on the utility of ethnic identity for the maintenance of community solidarity.[5] Essentially, then, it is evident that a community may be viewed and interpreted in a number of different ways and through the prism of diverse paradigms.

> ...The term embraces such factors as territoriality or spatial distribution, and human aggregates who share common experiences, value systems, and social institutions...it also connotes power distribution...associational character and friendship cliques.[6]

THE VILLAGE combines a number of the features attributed to "a community" in the descriptions discussed so far. THE VILLAGE approaches a *gemeinschaft*, a status not totally achieved primarily due to the subtle influences of locational proximity to a huge metropolis, Cleveland, Ohio.

In this volume on THE VILLAGE, the focus is not simply on a characterization of community life; it is a gallant effort to employ oral history and the traditions of ethnography to "correct omissions in the history of Afro-Americans" in metropolitan Cleveland, especially their political history, and to demonstrate how "race related beliefs and values about the nature of society intrude in the conduct of inquiry...."

THE VILLAGE refers to a subarea of "old Miles Heights," a small land area, adjacent to Cleveland, populated by a small settlement of Black Americans, Italians and Germans as early as 1913. However, the focal point is the social construction of reality as it affects the social and political experiences of the Black settlers in this small geographical area. The impetus for this study emerged from the "stories" Watson "heard from his parents and elders while growing up in 'old Miles Heights'." He heard the story of a Black man who had served as mayor of this small town long before Carl Stokes became the first Black to serve as Mayor of a major interracial city in the United States. He also heard "stories" about patterns of social relationships, the formation and functions of social institutions, the difficulties of sustaining life in an environment in which economic poverty appeared normative, and of the way "things used to be" when "everyone was family." This curiosity about "old Miles Heights" led him to explore further the methodological tools of oral history, historiography, ethnography; archival searches, and content analysis, as well as face-to-face interviews as ways of "reconstructing social reality" and correcting misconceptions about the political history of Blacks in metropolitan Cleveland.

One of the more salient findings resulting from Watson's prodigious research and through his discussions with "elder" informants, natives of "old Miles Heights", was the discovery that Arthur R. Johnston was the first Black to serve as an elected mayor of a predominantly white political district in Cuyahoga County, Ohio. Serving between 1929 and 1931 (for a period of three years), Johnston preceded Carl B. Stokes by some thirty eight years. Watson's discussion of the ascendancy of Johnston to the mayoralty demonstrates the salience and power of "the Black vote" and its pivotal position in crucial elections. It also demonstrates that power is not only a function of such factors as social organization, expertise, or charisma, but also may be a product of behavioral or personal attributes that characterize an individual. Watson reminds us that the election of a Black person to the top echelons of political leadership does not, ipso facto, result in direct benefits to Black people. Benefits, whatever they are, must be shared by all constituents. Moreover, the quantity of benefits is dictated by political, economic, and social resources prevalent within the community and the manner in which the political leadership organizes or mobilizes them for redistribution to community members. That allocation of resources may be limited by forces external to the immediate community itself (e.g., a worldwide economic depression).

Watson's discussion of the institutional infrastructure of THE VILLAGE is in the tradition of such pioneer American community studies as the Lynds[7] influential Middletown research. He examines the "everyday life" of the people of THE VILLAGE, their patterns of social interaction, lifestyles, economic activity, family structure, religious organization, patterns of schooling and the role of the school in the community, health care, self-help instrumentalities and belief systems related to self-help, and cultural changes taking place within the community over the study period.

In THE VILLAGE, family life was characterized by mutual support and adherence to an ethic of reciprocity. As one person put it, "if one person eats, everybody eats." As observed in primary groups in the main, a strong sense of neighborliness prevailed, and informal mechanisms of social control operated to minimize public display of disharmony among family members. It is assumed that the situations and relationships found among family groups in the Black community were observed also among the Italian and German sectors of the population since racial antagonisms were not widespread. Hence, adults, in general, disciplined the young, and child-rearing was shared by older persons, including those outside the immediate family of origin or the family of procreation. While ethnic solidarity was evident among the three ethnic groups within THE VILLAGE and although marriages tended to be endogamous, no apparent social ostracism was experienced by persons who married exogamously. The typical dyad of interracial marriages consisted of a minority male and a white female. Persons who married exogamously were integrated socially into the community and family structures.

People in THE VILLAGE were poor. As a consequence of poverty, neighbors found it necessary to share, to be mutually supportive and to seize opportunities that facilitated an escape from poverty. Boxing professionally was one avenue of escape from poverty. Watson provides prominent examples of individuals who were successful in that endeavor and who became a source of community pride.

Social bonds were strengthened by informal neighborhood gatherings and through various reunions of members or former members of social clubs. Picnics and reunions brought together persons whose ties to the community were so strong that even those who had emigrated to somewhat distant communities often would return and rekindle long-established social relations.

Small communities in close proximity to large urban or metropolitan areas often find it difficult if not impossible to retain "their sense of community" since they cannot resist the forces of culture contact and the kinds of social change generated by proximity and contact. For instance, while THE VILLAGE often lacked many of the amenities associated with a modernized city, such as public transportation, indoor plumbing, and electricity, the process of technological change resulting from desires and demands for annexation almost inevitably created situations which led to "a loss of community." Watson informs the reader that "improvements in public utilities, roads, and business development" engendered new strains on older families and changes in social customs, and threatened the loss of community. Yet, a sense of community, attachments, and social bonds persisted among many persons who left the geographical area of THE VILLAGE.

The sense of community, in a purely social-psychological framework, was manifested further in such activities as "taking up collections" for the needy, or for people without sufficient burial insurance and funds to bury deceased family members. It was present in the strategies devised to cope with other forms of adversity, strategies such as caring for the sick and infirm, searching for a physician or a midwife, or using home remedies to treat the ill when a physician could not be found, or when scientific medical procedures seemed dysfunctional.

The church and the school were important social institutions in THE VILLAGE. Watson points to a number of sources to support his contention that "religious beliefs and practices have been essential features of everyday life" in Afro-American communities. The church is an integral part of the family and is supportive, if not always a surrogate, of traditional family functions. Just as the "hawker" peddler is the source of information and a purveyor of news, so is the church a meeting place for strengthening social relations, communication bonds, entertainment and the sharing of news of special interest to community members. Watson is careful to document the historical development and interrelationships between the major religious groups that settled in THE VILLAGE. He clearly demonstrates the fact that family groups often provided the major nucleus of church membership, and the leadership of these religious bodies as well. Hence, in a structural sense, the interrelationship between family and church often was profound. In total, Watson points to some ten major functions of the church in THE VILLAGE and, thus, in most Black communities in America.

A major strength of this volume is the manner in which Watson captures the flavor and tenor of village life or primary group relationships. Of special importance here is the example of the peddler as a form of private business enterprise. His treatment of the hawker is especially salient in this regard. The hawker shouts and hollers as he approaches a street or neighborhood. He is there not only to sell "blocks of ice, heating coal, fresh fruit and groceries including fresh meat, fish, and some dairy products"; the peddler, especially the hawker, is as well a repository of information about events occurring in other areas, a purveyor of information about family members, other neighbors, a person who transmits knowledge of value about community leaders. The hawker sells and visits and socializes with all with whom he makes contact. He was not an innocent by-stander in the daily life of the community but a significant part of it while engaging in entrepreneurial activities.

Finally, Watson's discussion on "the social construction of social history" is especially illuminating and highly informative. He attacks head on the "problems of historiography and interpretation, and the uses to which historical interpretations are put." He reminds us once again that there are several determinants of who and what become the subject of social inquiry. These factors are explored amply in Chapter 8. In the main, this study of THE VILLAGE is an important contribution to the sociology of knowledge and to a long series of community studies.

James E. Blackwell
University of Massachusetts/Boston
October 1988

PREFACE

...The phenomena of society are worth the most careful and systematic study, and whether or not this study may eventually lead to a systematic body of knowledge deserving the name of science, it cannot in any case fail to give the world a mass of truth worth the knowing....(Dubois, 1971).[1]

The focus of this study is a small settlement of African American people, primarily migrants from the rural Southeastern United States, who established residence in a small land area in Warrensville Township, Ohio, at least as early as 1913. Of special concern is the important but previously undocumented history of political and economic achievements and the social organization and culture of these early twentieth century newcomers to the northeastern Ohio area. This small predominantly black community will be referred to as "THE VILLAGE," the folk name given the settlement by the black residents.

One of the noteable but not well known historical features of THE VILLAGE, that is a subdivision of old Miles Heights is that it produced the first black elected Mayor of a politically and economically autonomous district in the history of Ohio. While that mayor, Arthur R. Johnston, had a shortlived term, about 3 years or 1 1/2 terms (1929-1931), he was nevertheless distinguished by preceding by 38 years Carl

B. Stokes, Mayor of Cleveland, 1967-1971, as the first black elected Mayor of a predominantly white political district within Cuyahoga County, Ohio.

It is widely known that by winning election to the office of Mayor in the 1960s, Stokes became the first African American to head one of the largest predominantly white cities in the United States. It is also true that, according to the *Negro Almanac* of 1983, there were 206 black mayors in the United States by April of 1982.[2] While the achievements of Stokes and numerous other mayors are well documented in social science texts, specialized monographs, and reference books, Johnston and his achievements have been almost entirely ignored by scholars.

To help correct these omissions in the history of Afro-Americans, a part of this book is focused in detail on the mayoralty of Arthur R. Johnston. In addition, this study closely examines the social and cultural history of THE VILLAGE, that predominantly black section of old Miles Heights where Johnston and his family lived. It is through a study of the history and customs of the people of THE VILLAGE, of which the Johnston family was an integral part, that an appreciation of the magnitude of Johnston's achievements and of his place and that of THE VILLAGE in the history of African Americans in Ohio will develop.

The history of African Americans and revisionist histories thereof in the United States is one of the most extensively scrutinized bodies of knowledge among modern social scientists and their students.[3] In addition to its ethnographic content and contribution to community studies, this book makes

THE VILLAGE xvii

a threefold contribution to Afro-American history or the broad area of "black studies" and the sociology of community studies: (1) by documenting the mayoralty of Arthur R. Johnston, this study achieves a revision of the political history of African Americans in Cleveland and Ohio; (2) by adding detailed documentation on "old Miles Heights" and THE VILLAGE within, both of which have been omitted from texts and specialized works on the history of blacks in Cleveland and Ohio, a broader perspective on the social history of African Americans in Cleveland and Ohio is achieved; and (3) through a detailed discussion of "the social construction of social history," knowledge is advanced about ways in which values, beliefs and special interests help to determine the contents of records that become representations of the social history and stock of knowledge of a people.

Many sources were used to reconstruct the history of THE VILLAGE and the political career of Johnston. Oral historical records were collected through in-depth interviews with VILLAGE elders, some of whom still reside in the area and lived there during the first half of the twentieth century. The use of oral historical interviews was largely compelled by the absence of accurate census data and other documents about THE VILLAGE and its population before 1925. Social, political, economic, and other historical materials which focus on the social development of the immediate area, the City of Cleveland, Cuyahoga County, Miles Heights village, Bedford, Ohio, and Garfield Heights, Ohio and general histories of the State of Ohio were used as secondary sources to reconstruct the early history of THE VILLAGE.

Oral Historical Analysis as Telling Stories About Story Tellers

In addition to the contributions of this book to revising the history of African Americans in Ohio, the study is methodologically important in its use of story telling, as rendered by elderly informants, as a means of revealing, reconstructing, and preserving culture. This is a well established technique in folklore and cultural anthropology that is widely used to reveal and document the cultures of peoples worldwide.[4] Much less, however, has this technique been used systematically by social scientists to study the cultures and cultural histories of blacks in the United States. Notable exceptions to the foregoing conclusion are the earlier works by Davis, Gardner, and Gardner on *Deep South*;[5] works by Hurston, such as *Tell My Horse*;[6] Hughes and Bontemps' *Book of Negro Folklore*,[7] and the more recent studies by Kennedy on black family life in Mississippi,[8] Gwalthney's "Self Portrait of Black America,"[9] and Krech's study of "The Life of Joseph L. Sutton."[10]

The aim is to reconstruct or reveal, as much as possible, the history and culture of a previously isolated and neglected people through the verifiable information that they give about themselves. Most important are the insights given by indigenous oral historians, informants as it were--mostly elders but also some youthful members of the community. Also significant are observations of land use patterns; household and family organization; observable behavior in institutional settings, such as churches, and settings for the exchange of economic goods and services. Collectively, these varying sources of data provide the details needed to tell the

THE VILLAGE xix

full story of the history and sociocultural organization of a people.[11] In addition to developing accurate and detailed records about the stories told by individual informants, an attempt is made to interpret the deeper meanings of these stories, such as the assumptions on which observations, arguments, and judgements are based; the proclaimed and implied values, beliefs, and rules for behavior in the everyday lives of the people, their fears and occasions of euphoria, and their sense of control or lack thereof over environmental forces.[12] It is in the process of unpacking the deeper meanings of what people say about themselves by interpreting, first those sayings in terms of archives and other records of their cultural history; and second the interpretation of these materials within the broader contexts of other societies, cultures, and social science theory that those parts of this book focusing on the analysis of oral historical and other ethnographic materials can be construed as telling stories about story tellers. Chapter Seven develops a detailed discussion of approaches to the study of history with special reference to uses of oral historical data.

Historical records available in the libraries of the Western Reserve Historical Society and in the office of the Recorder for the City of Cleveland, Ohio provided demographic and settlement data on VILLAGE inhabitants after 1925. These archives were studied in addition to the oral historical records developed and analyzed for four generations of VILLAGERS who inhabited this settlement at the time of the study, or who lived there at one time or another in the years past. To determine the accuracy of any conclusions drawn from the analyses of oral historical and other kinds of data, such as census and city records, each source was checked for its validity by comparisons with other information that was claimed to be, or reasonably could be assumed to be, an accurate factual representation of the history, social organization, and culture of THE VILLAGE.

Acknowledgements

Numerous people, places, and events helped to stimulate my imagination and the unbending passion to pursue the research that culminated in this book. Foremost among them were the rich and challenging experiences that I had growing up in THE VILLAGE. My father, Lovest Lee Watson (deceased, November 9, 1986); my mother, Marjorie Christine Watson; my maternal grandmother, Canary Williford, and paternal grandmother, Mary Lou Watson were foremost among the individuals who guided my growth and in many ways, without knowing it, planted the seeds of the questions which stimulated my imagination early on in this inquiry. I also thank my sister and other family and kin for being encouraging and supportive throughout this project.

Many years after beginning my inquiry on Johnston and THE VILLAGE, I had the fortune of meeting Constance Parton and Leola Fantroy, the surviving daughters of Arthur R. Johnston. In addition to encouraging me to go on with my study and writing of the story of THE VILLAGE, they provided me access to personal documents that helped to answer questions and fill lacunae about their father that were previously unknown and/or undocumented.

Douglass Mitchell, Director of the University of Chicago Press, provided useful criticism and recommendations for improvement of an earlier draft. Among colleagues in the social sciences, I am grateful to Paula Dressel, Georgia State University, Eleanor Krassen Maxwell, University of North Carolina at Wilmington, and David Dorsey and Hubert Ross, Clark Atlanta University for careful readings of an early draft of the entire manuscript and for recommending substantive as well as stylistic changes in my writing. I am also grateful to Irving Louis Horowitz for comments and constructive criticism on my early writing and the anonymous referees of Village Vanguard Press whose comments, criticisms, and recommended improvements helped considerably to improve the manuscript.

A special thanks is due James E. Blackwell, University of Massachusetts. I am especially grateful to him for taking the time to read my manuscript and write the Foreword. His perspective helps to show the place of THE VILLAGE within the broader context of community studies in the social sciences and African Americans in the history of the United States. Secondly, his early writing on *Black Community: Unity And Diversity* raised several research questions that periodically were recalled for reflection during the course of my inquiry. While I do not fully agree with his analysis, his published thought on community studies was helpful in the formulation of my own point of view and is credited in various places in the book.

Toward the end of my writing, Beverly Guy Sheftall, Spelman College (Women's Resource and Research Center), and Mrs. Lucy C. Grigsby, Atlanta University, provided helpful tips on how to improve my writing style and other features of the manuscript. I also thank John McKenzie, the

Stein Printing Company (Atlanta), for his advice on graphics and production of selected visual illustrations used in the text.

In ways in which they may have not yet come to realize, my children, Stephen and Sheryl, also provided incentives for me to pursue and finish this work. I wanted them, their children, and their children's children to know as much as possible about their family heritage. This is a contribution to that end. Although previously I had told them, orally, much that is now written in these pages, undocumented and unrecorded oral historical accounts are not as lasting, convincing, nor conducive to review and re-analysis as the printed word. Secondly, their willingness to talk with me, or simply to be good listeners at times when I wanted to discuss the research provided much needed support.

Finally, I am grateful to all of the typists and word processor operators who have assisted me on the numerous drafts of this manuscript over the years. Since my coming to Atlanta University in 1980, Ms. Hattie S. Bell, Priscilla Smalls, and Jill Spencer have been especially helpful. A special thanks goes to Ms. Carol E. Johnson for her technical skills in desktop publishing. As often occurs in writing projects like this one, some errors tend to remain in the final printing of the manuscript. I accept full responsibility for whatever shortcomings are found.

CHAPTER 1

INTERFACES OF AUTOBIOGRAPHY AND SOCIAL HISTORY

> My Father stands with me in a We-relation and his childhood experiences, while antedating my birth, are nevertheless experiences of a fellowman of mine, although they carry a subscript of historicity. Yet they properly belong to the world of my predecessors because I cannot coordinate past phases of my own conscious life with these experiences of my fellow-man. Such past direct and indirect experiences of social reality on the part of my fellow-man therefore belong to a genuinely past domain of the social world, but I gain knowledge of it through the mediation of communicative acts in a genuine We-or They-relation (Schutz, 1974).[1]

My initial exposure to the history of old Miles Heights occurred during my late childhood through folktales told by my father and other old timers. Telling folktales was a favorite pasttime in old Miles Heights.

Many stories focused on the hardships suffered by blacks during slavery and problems of reconstruction during the late nineteenth century. The exodus of blacks from the South during and since World War I also provided substance for story telling. Descriptions of stereotypes and expressive behavior of whites toward blacks; ways in which blacks made fun of whites and how "whites made fools of themselves"; and means by which blacks attempted to protect each other from the abusive behaviors of whites were recurrent themes in these stories. It was through these folktales that I got my first glimpse of the multiple meanings and tragedies of racism and discriminatory treatment of blacks under the rules of racial separatism in public accomodations such as segregated lunch counters, water fountains, schools, and other facilities. I remember as a child my own feelings of fear and anger as I listened, more than once, to accounts of lynchings of blacks by hooded night riders; how my father and his brothers and sisters, their parents and other members of the family left Greenville, Georgia (my father's birthplace) under the cover of darkness and headed North for fear of losing their lives to a marauding band of Klansmen. Yet, all tales were not pessimistic nor focused on the South.

My father, who was known as "Love," regularly took his turn at story telling. One of his favorite stories was about a black "gun tottin" man named Arthur R. Johnston who, according to Love, was Mayor of old Miles Heights during the late 1920s. Because of Johnston's popularity, stories about him were told frequently and heard by me until my early adult years when I left home to pursue full-time undergraduate studies at Kent State University.

During my college years, I undertook several fruitless searches of the social science literature hoping to find historical documents about Johnston and old Miles Heights. With growing frustration, I began to question the truth value of the folktales about A.R. Johnston and old Miles Heights. Before giving up, however, I spent some time during the Summer of 1970 studying the archives of the old *Cleveland Press* and *Cleveland Plain Dealer*. I looked through numerous old newspaper clippings for stories of any kind about old Miles Heights. This effort bore fruit. The excerpt from the *Cleveland Plain Dealer*, December, 1929, printed at the opening of Chapter Three, was one of the products of my search.

Old Miles Heights was a small town in comparison to Cleveland, whose Mayor's Office was won by Carl B. Stokes in 1967. In many ways, the challenges faced by Johnston in 1928 were pale in comparison to those faced by Stokes as Mayor of one of the largest cities in the United States. There is no claim, however, of comparability of scale nor tasks faced by Stokes and Johnston.

Johnston's achievements are significant for other reasons. Important as his success was in winning electoral office, he was also a folk hero rising to the mayoralty of a village with a predominantly white population during a social historical period in the United States when racial separatism was sanctioned both legally and culturally, a challenge that Stokes did not have to face in the late 1960s. As Drake and Cayton observed[2] in their study of outstanding blacks in Chicago during the period of separatism:

> If a man is an aggressive, vocal, uncompromising Race Man he is everybody's hero. Even conservative Negroes admire colored radicals who buck the white

world....Race pride sometimes verges upon the vindictive, but it is a direct result of the position to which white America has consigned the Negro group.

Secondly, Johnston provided leadership and at least symbolic protection for the black inhabitants of THE VILLAGE, many of whom only recently had fled the deep South for what LeRoi Jones called "Jordan,"[3] a metaphor of hope variously symbolized by "jobs, homes, and dignity" in the "promised land" north of the Mason-Dixon Line as well as an escape from racist oppression and brutality that was so pervasive in the South at the turn of the century. Many blacks who fled the South, including VILLAGERS, were to find later that their new Northern neighbors often confronted them with racial barriers as formidable as their previous experiences in the South and elsewhere.[4]

It was the widespread oppression of blacks under separatism, especially that symbolized by racial segregation in public accomodations; reports of physical brutality and lynching,[5] and only scattered accounts of individuals or groups who had had any success in thwarting the degradation of blacks by whites that made the Johnston story and his political successes so compelling. Secondly, my finding of only a small number of newspaper accounts of Johnston's life and times with no detailed treatment by historians of the period intensified the importance of culling from the historical record details about Johnston and THE VILLAGE and attempting to revise public understanding of African Americans in the history of Cleveland, Ohio.

The previous absence of documentation of the life, times and achievements of Johnston; the ignorance and/or lack of recognition accorded him by historians raised several questions in my mind: (1) How does ethnic group identity, class background, ideological stance and other factors bear on the work of the historiographer?,[6] and (2) In a racially stratified society like the United States how do race-related beliefs and values about the nature of society intrude in the conduct of inquiry to determine the development of archives, historiographic and other kinds of social science investigations?[7] During the course of the study of THE VILLAGE, these questions and a variety of others were posed recurrently by me as new insights emerged from the research. While there is no pretense that this study gives fully satisfactory answers to any of these questions, some tentative conclusions are set forth in the essays that form the body of the book, especially Chapter Eight on the "Social Construction of Social History."

In addition to the broad focus on historiography and the social construction of social history, a major part of this book is addressed to ways in which these Afro-Americans learned to cope with the exigencies of everyday life in spite (or because) of the racially separatist society that formed the social and political economic context of THE VILLAGE in which they eked out their existence. Through the oral histories and ethnographic accounts of everyday life, details emerge about ways in which the people pooled their resources in family, church, health care, and economic exchange. Materials are also presented on interactions between VILLAGE insiders and outsiders; the development of small businesses, beginning immediately following World War I; and a variety of other social, political, and economic changes that occurred up through the decade of the 1980s.

The growing interaction between the City of Cleveland and THE VILLAGE since the l930s has changed structurally the institutions, boundaries, and everyday lives of the people. Because of the importance of historiography in this study, and the differing perspectives on social history in the literature, I will take an aside, before proceeding, to set forth the particular point of view on social history used in this study.

Social History as Accomplished Events and as a Social Construct

History as a naturalistic process, something that happens "out there," as it were, may be construed as accomplished events, some singular, others in sequence, which may or may not have left traces like footsteps in the sand; or may or may not have been recorded systematically by observers.[8] As a discipline whose practitioners are concerned with the objective development of recordable sequences of events and systematic analyses of the contents and outcomes thereof, history can be construed as a relatively rigorous area of inquiry characterized by the same problems of objectivity, measurement, and explanation as the other social sciences. However, as suggested by Schutz in his essay on "The World of Predecessors and the Problem of History"[9] and Berger and Luckman,[10] "reality is socially constructed" and is, in part, constituted by the accounts made of social history.

In his essay on "objective possibility and adequate causation in historical explanation," Weber reached a similar conclusion:

> The first step towards an historical judgement is a process of abstraction. This process proceeds through the analysis and mental isolation of the components of the directly given data--which are to be taken as a complex of possible causal relations--and should culminate in a synthesis of the 'real' causal complex. Even this first step thus transforms the given 'reality' into a mental construct' in order to make it into an historical fact. In Goethe's words, "theory" is involved in the "fact."[11]

In the study of THE VILLAGE, social history was conceived as socially constructed patterns of interaction over times past having occurred between individuals and groups whose relations were regulated by systems of values, beliefs and rules for social behavior relatively specific to the social historical period of the generation of interaction partners. The empirical indicators of these phenomena were isolated and documented through archival records of accomplished events and oral historical accounts.

It should be noted that the concern in the study of THE VILLAGE was not merely the unfolding of social relations and culture change as objectifiable historical events and processes. This study also focused on the association between culture change and change in social relations among group members. It is in the sense that change in culture represents change in social relations, even though to some extent received culture constrains the process of social change, that the position is taken here that accounts of social history are social reconstructions of historical reality, not merely objective records or documentaries of past social and cultural events. Constraint of culture on social change is shown, for example, in each new generation's uses of received categories of thought to describe and interpret the world of its predecessors and to forecast future possiblities. This point of view is consistent with Mannheim's analysis of "the nature of facts."

> They exist for the mind always in an intellectual and social context. That they can be understood and formulated implies already the existence of a conceptual apparatus. And if this conceptual apparatus is the same for all the members of a group, the presuppositions (i,e., the possible social and intellectual values), which underly the individual concepts never become perceptible.... However, once the unanimity is broken, the fixed categories which used to give experience its reliable and coherent character undergo an inevitable disintegration. There are divergent and conflicting modes of thought which (unknown to the thinking subject) order the same facts of experience into different systems of thought, and cause them to be

perceived through different logical categories.[12]

When set against the background of previous historical accounts of blacks in Ohio, this study of THE VILLAGE clearly represents a break from the perspectives and conclusions that heretofore represented Ohio history. Moreover, the new findings presented in this study introduce a conflicting perspective on the history of blacks in Cleveland from 1913 to 1980, and calls for a revision in the textbook writings about events that occurred during those years of Cleveland's and Ohio's histories.

Before closing this discussion, I will comment briefly on Mead's[13] perspective on "time" and its pertinence to our subject. Mead saw the sociotemporal period of the conduct of research as a factor that conditions the perceptions and conclusions of the investigator in the research process. My revelation of the mayoralty of Johnston and the argument for a revision of the history of African Americans in Cleveland may be judged through future inquiry to be a 1988 account of a "present" in 1929 that had a past, including a black Mayor (perhaps in Cuyahoga County) earlier than Johnston, whose present was not recorded in the archives or oral histories made available to me during my research and writing. Moreover, the omission of the Johnston Mayoralty will almost certainly not be the only error found in other revisionist histories of Afro-Americans in Cleveland. Depending on the value premises brought by future historians to this area of inquiry, it may not be perceived as as significant an omission as other events or errors not yet discovered.[14]

Overview

To clearly establish THE VILLAGE in space and time, the next Chapter, on "Everybody was Family," describes the setting, family migration and settlement in the area, selected customs, and folk heroes as told to me by VILLAGE Informants. Attention is drawn to the significance of family life and close ties, and mutual support among members of THE VILLAGE. Through a close examination of folk heroes, key aspects of the values and beliefs of the VILLAGERS are revealed.

As already established, one of the most important folk heroes was Arthur R. Johnston. His major distinction was the achievement of the mayoralty of old Miles Heights. Because of the historical importance of Johnston and previous neglect in the social science literature of his political achievements, an entire chapter, number Three, is devoted to his life and times. The discussion develops insight into the social and political context of the period of his run for political office and the term of his mayoralty, his family life and concern that government be devoid of corruption, selected economic and political problems of his administration, difficulties faced in keeping the schools open in the early years of the depression of the 1930s, the annexation of Miles Heights to the City of Cleveland, and Johnston's career thereafter.

Following the discussion of Johnston's life and times, a close look is taken at the everyday life of the people in relation to health care (Chapter 4), the church (Chapter 5), economic activity (Chapter 6), and other domains of social relations. These chapters help to show the bearing of strong determinations to overcome adversity, such as poverty and social isolation, on the development of mutually supportive relationships among community members.

Chapter Eight contains a more detailed discussion of the social construction of social history. The aim is to recast the issues about selectivity in recording and storing documents about historical events in a broader analytic framework. In particular the focus is the social structure of decision making in social research: Emphasis is put on the problems of ethnocentrism, gender, and political bias. There is also a discussion of the nature of the oral historical interview, its significance in the reconstruction of historical events, and the problem of developing reliable techniques for culling accurate indepth information from older informants whose recall about their lived experiences and other events past may be questionable.

Against the background of this overview, let us enter THE VILLAGE proper. The focus will be on the setting and the people: First, "Everybody was Family."

CHAPTER 2

EVERYBODY WAS FAMILY

The soul of a city is in the relations among its people (Pope John Paul II, New York Times, 1979).[1]

"Everybody was a family out here. If one person eats, everybody eats. You didn't have to lock your door. Everybody looked out for everybody else (Addie Crosby-Jackson)."[2]

"When it came to discipline, anybody could discipline you. Rearing children was shared among families. Everybody tended to protect each other and anybody from outside THE VILLAGE was thought of as a threat and they were set upon if they did anything half way wrong. THE VILLAGE was like a society that protected itself and kept everybody else out (Johnell Gresham)."[3]

If the soul of a community is in the relations among its people, then the soul of THE VILLAGE was deeply sensitive, humanistic and mutually supportive. This was especially the case with attitudes expressed among in-group members toward each other. These qualitites of the relations among the people of THE VILLAGE were symbolized in a variety of ways, especially in ethnic group relationships, attitudes toward interracial marriages, peer group ties, annual reunions among current and former VILLAGERS, and commumnity response to death among the poor in the VILLAGE. In the pages that follow, the qualities of sensitivity, humanistic concern and mutually supportive relationships in the everyday lives of the people of THE VILLAGE will be discussed.

Early Settlers

Dating the earliest settlers of old Miles Heights is difficult. According to some accounts, parts of the area may have been settled by "squatters" as early as 1900.[4] Other old timers said that between 1900 and 1920 approximately 80 black families moved to and settled in the area. However, due to the marshy or swampy conditions and a lack of land clear of trees, along with heavy growth of other vegetation, most of the families lived in one and two room "shanties" constructed from any available materials that would help to provide housing, at least temporarily.[5] The inhabitants during this period lived very close together. Other than newcomers who sought to become members of the settlement, outsiders were not permitted idle passage, such as vagrancy, nor were they necessarily welcome as unappointed visitors.

Most of the early settlers of THE VILLAGE arrived in small family groups. Perhaps because of the harsh living conditions and the lack of secondary institutions such as established churches, health care facilities, and other kinds of public agencies to which unattached adults could turn in times of need, there were no known single person households in this small community, except widows and widowers, and no single occupancy hotels or boarding houses until after World War II. While most families arrived intact in THE VILLAGE, in some cases members came to live with relatives who had arrived already. But the poverty level and low skills that characterized most newcomers along with the absence of job opportunities led many families to develop businesses based upon the few skills they had, or that could be cultivated among members. When pooled, these skills enabled them to make a living. For example, the Anthony family from Indiana and Tennessee brought with it skills in lath work, plastering, and other crafts of carpentry.[6] These skills were put to use through fee-for-service construction of housing for newcomers within and outside THE VILLAGE. According to one member of this family and several old timers who were familiar with their work, the Anthonys were responsible for the construction of at least ten wood frame homes in THE VILLAGE between 1928 and 1940, and possibly as many as 15.[7]

The Oatman family that will be discussed further in other parts of this study also had several members who were skilled in masonry, brick and block work, and the retail sale of goods and services. This family owns and still operates one of the oldest general stores in THE VILLAGE. This small family-owned and managed business that is known simply as Oatman's Store has operated continously since 1933. One of the key features of the family-owned businesses in THE VILLAGE was the employment opportunities that each made available for its own family members and relatives. While this practice did not always yield the greatest productivity or profits, it did help to lessen the economic suffering of many, paved the way for newcomers to establish roots, and gave them a sense of belonging upon their arrival among other settlers, often strangers, outside their family circle.

Ethnic Diversity and Origins of Migration

Some oral historical accounts place Afro-American, Italian, and German settlers in the area as early as 1913.[8] Among early Afro-American settlers a man named William Dark was said to have migrated to THE VILLAGE from Greenville, Georgia and settled there before World War I.[9] By 1913, Dark had built a small one-room house on the banks of a swamp in THE VILLAGE. Other early Afro-American settlers and housing developers before 1920 included Edna Lee, located putatively before 1913 on Ohio Avenue;[10] Gilbert Anthony, in 1918, on East 144th Street;[11] Arthur R. and Annabell Johnston, in 1919 on East 147th Street;[12] and Edgar and Esther Withers, on East 147th Street.[13]

Among the early Italian families, the Provateirs, the Cardimans and others were included. Perhaps it was the Italian influence that led to the early naming of THE VILLAGE as "Belle Villa." According to William Anthony, a 72-year-old informant and early settler, Belle Villa was the name commonly used to refer to the geographical area of THE VILLAGE (outlined in Plate Number 2.1) before its incorporation as part of Miles Heights village in 1927.[14] Also shown in

THE VILLAGE

Plate Number 2.1, Miles Heights village subsumed Belle Villa or the area that is referred to in this study as THE VILLAGE.

Based upon the oral historical interviews of old timers, most of the early settlers of THE VILLAGE migrated there from the southern United States. However, a sizeable number, including the family of Arthur R. Johnston, had settled in various sectors of inner city Cleveland, such as the Mt. Pleasant area, before moving to old Miles Heights.

States of origin of early migrants included Georgia, Alabama, Mississippi, Tennessee, Kentucky, Indiana, South and North Carolina, and Virginia. The motives of these peoples for leaving their home states and moving to Cleveland, THE VILLAGE, and other northern residential areas were varied. Poverty and the search for economic opportunity through the war works industries, white oppression and abuses of blacks, including hangings and castration of males, and feelings of powerlessness to alter these practices were among the motives for outmigration from various southern states. The following quote from an oral historical interview of an early settler is illustrative:

> "I had come from Georgia. [Many colored were] hateful because they [whites] used to hang colored men in Georgia, castrate them and do everything else! Put a [colored] man behind a plow and let him pull a plow like a mule pulls

Plate 2.1

The Boundaries of Miles Heights Village
When it was annexed to the City of Cleveland, 1932

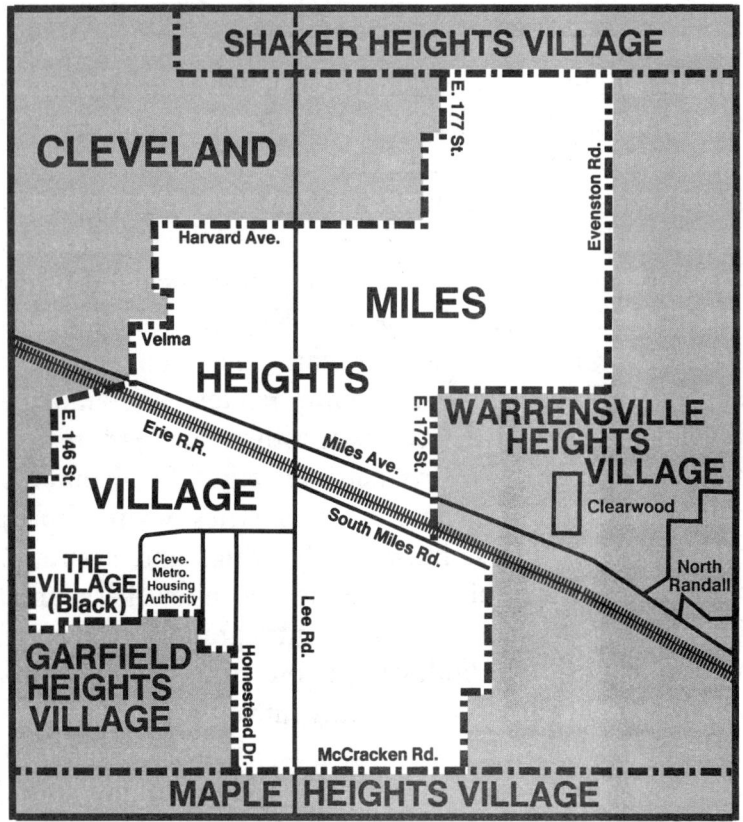

*Source: This map was drawn by John Mckenzie, 1988 Stein Printing Company, Atlanta, Georgia. The boundaries of Miles Heights Village are based upon an aerial photo of the area in the *Cleveland Plain Dealer*, March 29, 1932. The boundaries of THE VILLAGE "(black)" are based upon a site visit by Wilbur H. Watson in 1986.

it. That's what the man does to the Negro. They used to castrate a colored man. Make him big and strong like you do hogs when you're fattening them up; getting ready for a killing, so they could work the field. That ain't in the history is it? That I know about. I'd like to say, they [whites] didn't allow them [colored] to leave the South. In a lot of places, they [colored people] couldn't leave unless they sneaked away. And some of them [colored] would get mean and mad with them [whites]; they call em [colored] crazy when you go to fighten on em [whites] and wouldn't take the bull. They [whites] call em [colored] crazy and wouldn't mess with em, but uh, the average one of us was weak and scared and stayed a long time [in the South]. Course, they tell me, its a lot different there [in the South] now." [15]

While some black migrants from the South went directly to THE VILLAGE to live with relatives or friends who were already settled and who had invited and assisted them in abandoning sharecropping on southern plantations, others came through routes that were more indirect. For example, many black families found places of residence in inner City Cleveland upon first arriving in this part of northeastern Ohio.[16] Only later, then, did some move from the inner city regions to settle in THE VILLAGE in old Miles Heights and other settlements just outside the borders of Cleveland.

As already noted above, there were also Italian and German families living in THE VILLAGE between 1900 and 1920. While their origins are not clear, nor their motives for choosing THE VILLAGE as a place to settle, there was a relatively clear residential pattern in their settlement behavior. According to oldtimers, most Italian families set up their households in a common peripheral area to form a "line settlement," a series of households distributed along one or sometimes each side of a single street that was the southern border of Ohio Avenue (see the map of THE VILLAGE, Plate Number 2.2). At least as early as 1922, there were a half dozen or more Italian and German farming families with independent households and lands running from East 144th to 153rd street along Ohio Avenue.

All Italians, however, did not live in the line settlement. At least two of the earliest families (1922) had taken up households on the northern side of Ohio Avenue inside the sector of THE VILLAGE that was occupied predominantly by blacks. The father of one Italian family, the Provateirs, later became distinguished as one of the three police officers of Miles Heights village during the period of the mayoralty of Arthur R. Johnston.

Interracial Marriages

As in so many other African American settlements in the history of the United States, although illegal in some states up through the mid-twentieth century,[17] marriages and families in THE VILLAGE were not restricted to relations between African Americans. Three interracially married

THE VILLAGE 20

Plate 2.2

Street Boundaries of THE VILLAGE, 1917-1988

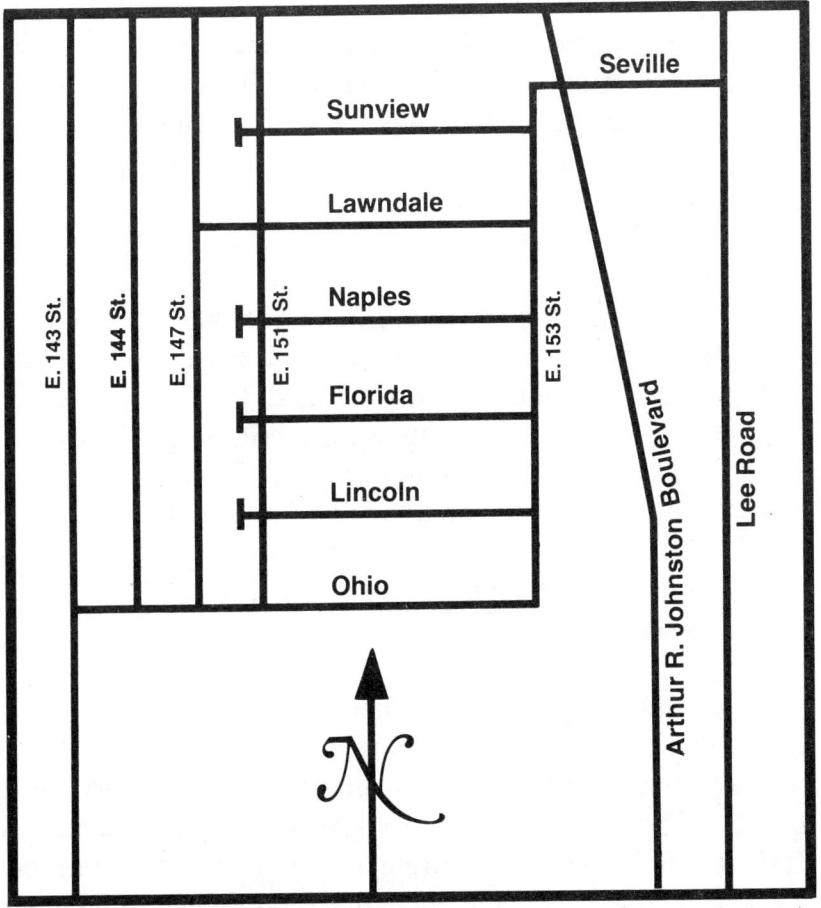

Source: This map was etched by John McKenzie, The Stein Printing Company, based upon a hand drawing by Marlene Leverette and Wilbur H. Watson following a site visit to THE VILLAGE in 1988.

couples were reported as early as the 1920s. "Spot" Gray, oneof the early settlers, was the first VILLAGER to cross the "color line" in marriage:

> "Spot Gray was the first black man we saw married to a white woman. That was the first time in my life I saw a Niggah doing something he wasn't supposed to do, and got away with it. Then, what it also meant to me was that protectionism of Miles Heights came into play: Miles Heights was an isolated island type place and within your own society you can do what you want to do if you can deal with it. What is so amazing to me (in looking back) was at that time, black folk accepted it; like it was o.k. You know, like Spot Gray had a white woman. You know at that time, you wasn't even supposed to talk about white women."[18]

According to some old timers, both women and men, these mixed couples were accepted and moved about freely in the community without any marked discriminatory treatment.[19] This finding parallels observations by Carpenter[20] in Buffalo, New York that during the same period interracial marriages were quite common. It should be noted, however, that both THE VILLAGE and the Buffalo findings diverged considerably from the broad customs pertaining to race and marriage in the United States society-at-large:

> The customs and norms of the white majority in the country, and to some extent the black minority, make interracial marriage a rare and deviant sort of behavior.
>
> Marriage among peoples of different cultural backgrounds is considered, by many students of assimilation, to be the ultimate test of the process of integration, as well as of whether a caste system exists, separating two peoples into superior and inferior beings. In these respects, then, the question of interracial marriage is more than a matter of personal choice; it is an index of the view and place of different peoples in the national life.[21]

In each interracial marital union in THE VILLAGE, the couple was composed of a black man married to a white woman. Among the informants interviewed for this study, no one assigned any special meaning to these pairs, nor suggested that they would have felt differently if the pairings had been the opposite, with black women married to white men.

Helping to show further the uniqueness of THE VILLAGE in this area of race relations is the observation of Schuman, Steeh, and Bobo in their recent book on *Racial Attitudes* in America: They found little improvement, nationally, in attitudes toward interracial marriage from 1940 to 1980 in the United States.[22] As suggested by Billingsley in the foregoing quotation, interracial marriage may be one of the most difficult areas to achieve integration between two racial groups that have been for centuries socially and culturally polarized and segregated as blacks and whites have been in the United States.

It was noted that the visibility of two of these white women was heightened through their "front stage" work as clerks at the checkout counters in the stores owned (or jointly owned) by their husbands. Their participation in the proprietorship of these successful businesses also enhanced their statuses and social acceptance in THE VILLAGE.[23]

Also worthy of note is the fact that no children were produced by these mixed couples. However, at least one member of each of two of these couples had had children through a previous marriage. In each case, these children of the latter unions were reared by the racially mixed couples.[24] Perhaps because of the broad acceptance of these interracial couples and their children in THE VILLAGE, the offspring reported no developmentally negative experiences as children of interracial couples, nor were there signs of maladjustment in adulthood.

The Crash of 1929 and the Coming of Pearl Harbor

As in towns large and small throughout the United States, the economic foundations of family and community in THE VILLAGE began to unravel after the economic crash of 1929. The effects of the Great Depression of the 1930's did not spare the people of the THE VILLAGE. Family life was harsh. Gainful employment was scarce. Partly due to the in-

THE VILLAGE 24

tense competition for jobs between blacks and whites in the industrial plants in Cleveland and Garfield Heights, race-related hostilities became widespread. Many black VILLAGERS who had left sharecropping and southern plantation life found themselves recreating images of their former lives and reliving experiences of the Southland past, especially in contacts with whites outside THE VILLAGE.

With the inception of the Work Projects Administration (1937), the development of war in Europe, the increasing activation of war works industries in the United States to support the Allies, and the subsequent entry of the United States into World War II in 1942, job opportunities increased. Like its effects on the economic growth of the entire United States, the expansion of war-related opportunities for work eventually helped to improve the employment and cash flow for VILLAGERS as well.

By the end of the war, some 14 years after annexation of old Miles Heights to the City of Cleveland, little had changed with respect to the living conditions in THE VILLAGE. Unpaved roads, open sewage ditches, outhouses for the elimination of human waste, homes without running water and open mosquito infested swamps were still present.

The return of war veterans and the effects of the post-war baby boom brought a demand for new housing. Massive federally supported public housing programs, new low-income housing projects with modern sanitation and storm sewers, as well as a small industrial park were constructed in the Lee-Seville area on land adjacent to THE VILLAGE. During the post-World-War-II period, this kind of development was seen in or on the periphery of many large cities with high concentrations of low income families in various parts of the United States. These land improvements on the periphery of THE VILLAGE stimulated expansion of the few small businesses that were in the original settlement as well as the development of new businesses, churches, street improvements and other city services.

With these improvements in public utilities, roads, and business development, new strains were brought to bear on the older families in THE VILLAGE. For the first time, THE VILLAGE was faced with the threat of a loss of community, of familiar faces and customs of old. Closely associated with the construction of new public housing projects in the 1940s and the influx of new residents, was a rise in the organization of small friendship groups and other kinds of bonds among VILLAGE oldtimers and their offspring. In addition to the close ties among members within these groups, the formation of these new intermediate groups strengthened ties among the older families that remained in THE VILLAGE.

Peer Group Ties

Small friendship groups and organized clubs played a major part in maintaining the social solidarity and the persistence of the spirit of THE VILLAGE. A good example of this phenomenon is the all male social club that formerly was known as the "Mystic Knights" (1950-72) and that currently is known as "The Nucleus" (1973-present).

> "The Nucleus was originally formed by a group of guys organized around the late Booker Telifero Leigh, founding President. They would gather at Booker's former residence, signify, drink, and talk stuff."[25]

> "Booker Leigh was like the father that we never had.... He was much older than we were. We looked upon him as a father and a peer. He would like to do the things for you that you wanted the father to do. Booker did those kinds of things because Booker loved you. Booker taught us, you know like, you're not just a little small time Miles Heights people, you're universal people. Booker was a big government man, working for the Veterans Administration and all that kind of stuff so he was kind of like, well-rounded about a lot of things. And Booker made himself available to us so we could vent feelings about things."[26]

The Nucleus is an organized group of 23 adult males ranging in age from 40 to 55, with educational levels ranging from high school diplomas to the Ph.D., D.D.S., and other terminal degrees. The members are all black, and all gainfully employed. The majority are also married and trace their family ties to old Miles Heights.

While only one member of The Nucleus still lived in THE VILLAGE in 1988, all of the members continue to meet monthly. Each gathering is focused upon the one factor held in common by all: Their pleasure in sharing humour and short stories about their life and times in THE VILLAGE. According to one of the founding members of The Nucleus:

> "It [The Nucleus] is a fraternity of older guys who have dealt with each other through a whole life time.... I think it's a group of people who are reliving some of the good Miles Heights things that have happened to us; and we've gotten through life, and we've accomplished things and we have still maintained ourselves. We still come together, and basically we are still like we were at The Center [a former place for teenage recreation in The VILLAGE operated by the City of Cleveland between 1950-58]. To me, it is the only organization I have ever been in that I can go back and relate to the past and bring it up [to the present] and see how we have all just like made this kind of crescent in life."[27]

Annual Reunion and Picnic of Families and Friends of VILLAGERS

Another response to the threat of loss of community that has functioned to maintain the spirit of THE VILLAGE is the annual "Miles Heights" reunion, an event that began in

1975 with a massive family picnic. This undertaking was developed through the interest of a number of current and former residents of THE VILLAGE. These persons had an interest in renewing ties among themselves, especially the social bond developed through their sentiments about THE VILLAGE, through which previously they were linked. The annual reunions that subsequently developed took two forms: a picnic once each year on Father's Day and a Reunion Dance once each year during the Christmas Holiday Season.

The first reunion was held in 1975 on Father's Day in Kerrush Park on Lee Road, a recreation facility on the southeastern periphery of THE VILLAGE (see Plate Number 2.2). About one hundred people showed up for this affair. As told by one of the organizers:

> "Not many people showed up for the first picnic, maybe a hundred. It was supposed to be like a picnic. A lot of people came with lunch; but people shared what they had. We ran out of beer, so we 'passed the hat.' And that was like a bond, like old times; everybody passed the hat and put in what they could to go for something to drink."[28]

Originally, the reunion was to be held on Memorial Day. However, Memorial Day in 1975 was too cold. The planners, who wanted this to be an annual affair, preferred a holiday time so that people would remember the occasion. Father's Day was chosen because it is always on a Sunday; it is a day when family members tend to do things together, and it occurs near the beginning of summer when the weather is usually warm and suitable for out-of-doors activities.

According to Stewart, one of the original organizers, the idea for the reunion grew out of youthful reminiscing about THE VILLAGE in earlier times; what it was like to grow up in its context, and a yearning by former and contemporary residents to renew periodically ties with old friends.[29]

> "There is a certain sense of brotherhood that I feel when I see so many good people that I know; that I've grown up with and respected over the years. And as they've grown up, they've contributed to society in terms of proper conduct and earning their own way, raising their kids. Then, haven't seen them in 15 or 20 years, and you kind of get a flashback on how you communicated by the way people are reacting to you.... And some of them will tell you. Then, there is the flip side. There is always a few people you don't want to see. They will, of course, remain nameless."[30]

To make the reunion appealing to young and old alike, the organizers decided to add dancing for the second year. Postcards and fliers were sent out so that everyone would know when and where to come. On the occasion of the first reunion dance, a hall was rented that would accommodate 400 people, although the organizers expected only 300. To their surprise, the actual attendance more than doubled expectations.

> "As it turned out, we must have gotten at least 800 in there, plus we had to have police protection. We had to lock the doors so no one else could come in. People were offering bribes to get in; 'I haven't seen my friend in twenty years' (said one man), 'let me in, let me in!'"[31]

The annual reunion dance, which occurs during the Christmas Holiday Season, has helped considerably to sustain a sense of oneness and solidarity among former VILLAGERS. The numbers of participants in this event have ranged from 400 to 800. To help pay the costs of a dance hall, refreshments, and a disc jockey, a nominal fee has been charged each participant. What is more significant is the interaction observed among VILLAGERS on these occasions.

At the entrance to the dance hall, the organizers placed dated photographs of classes of VILLAGERS who formerly attended Beehive School, the institution for public education which exclusively served the primary and secondary school needs of old Miles Heights from 1917 to 1932. While Beehive continued until 1980 to provide education for grades K-8, after the annexation of the Beehive School District to the Cleveland School District in 1932, other Cleveland public schools also became available to VILLAGERS.

Each photo of a class of students included its teacher. The class photos ranged from the first to the twelfth grade.

Not only did the display of photos draw attention as participants entered the dance hall, it immediately induced excited interaction associated with searches for self-identification and faces of old friends among the students in the photos.

> "To me, its like a sustaining thing. Like, what really sustains you? The past! Its like, you go back and draw on your past, and you say, this is good and this is bad, but I've gotta go ahead; I've gotta do this.... When I see Miles Heights reunions and I just go back and I think about my past, I think about what made me do what I did, or what made you do what you did, and man, we got a lot of very successful, good upstanding citizens who came out of Miles Heights. And it came because there was just some goodness, so fabric there that made people do what they want to do."[32]

Since 1975, the organizers of the Miles Heights reunions have met each year just before Father's Day. Out of these meetings have come plans to have an annual reenactment of the celebrations of THE VILLAGE described above. This kind of activity and the emotional uplift that it has given the participants has contributed considerably to the sense of belonging and the perpetuation of romantic imagery of THE VILLAGE.

Folk Heroes

Telling tales about folk heroes was another way of recalling and reinforcing ideals of VILLAGE life and cementing old and new ties among the people. A hero is a central figure admired for outstanding qualities or achievements representing character ideals of a society. The three heroes discussed here represent the following character ideals: (1) The tough risk-taking black who feared no man, especially no white. "Frog" was the folk name for the person representing this character. Along with others, Frog will be described below. (2) The artful pugilist who rose from THE VILLAGE streets, through the Golden Gloves, to a world bantamweight boxing championship. The Brooks family of the VILLAGE, of which all eight sons became Golden Glove competitors, also produced the archtype pugilist of THE VILLAGE. (3) Finally, there was the politically sophisticated African American VILLAGER (A.R. Johnston), who won election to the office of mayor of old Miles Heights. Each of these characters will be discussed in the order in which they were introduced.

Frog

Frog got his name from his short physical stature, short thick neck, bald head, and very dark complexion. Moreover, his eyes were often bloodshot and he spoke in a deep, crackling voice. But these were not the characteristics that brought Frog deference among THE VILLAGERS.

It will be recalled that the residents of THE VILLAGE have been predominantly black since 1927. Partly because of the predominant white and racist police force of the City of Cleveland that was seen with increasing frequency in THE VILLAGE after annexation in 1932, hostility toward the police developed among some VILLAGERS.

> "The two things that would be likely to draw the attention of police during that era was the fact that [Frog] was black, number one, and he didn't subordinate himself to the police. Just that fact alone in the 30s and 40s would draw the attention of police to any black if they had this knowledge. They could never approach him and get the proper deference from him.... It was known that he wouldn't buckle under."[33]

Because of his presence in THE VILLAGE, sometimes appearing as a vagrant, Frog became an individual whom policemen often attempted to arrest. But because of his "brute" strength and agility at fisticuffs, Frog was seldom easy prey. These were among the social, cultural, and individual attributes that earned Frog the admiration of young VILLAGERS.

> "He was one of the earliest blacks who represented a backbone such that the authorities had to at least prepare themselves before they just arbitrarily issued either decrees or took marked action against him. When an individual police officer knew he was dealing with Frog, he

knew he was dealing with somebody who wouldn't submit, number one, and number two, somebody he knew he probably couldn't subdue unless he uses his gun. So he [Frog] kind of made a statement; a statement that 'there is at least one black in this community who, when we go to get him, we have got to use sufficient force because we know he is not going to buckle under.' In a sense, Frog represented the same thing that the post-World-War-II veteran represented in a more positive sense. [That was] a certain manifest resolve; something whose omission has hampered blacks' positive development in terms of any credibility in American society to this day.... If blacks are ever going to be anything in America, they must stand up and not buckle under the system."[34]

The social significance of Frog in THE VILLAGE was related closely to the long history of racial oppression and exploitation of blacks by whites that many VILLAGERS had known firsthand in the "old country" (The rural South from which most had migrated) and in the VILLAGE itself. Moreover, while the police symbolized brute force and the authority of law in society-at-large, and thereby drew a measure of respect from VILLAGERS, like people in other communities,[35] they also stood for the odious strong arm of oppression and white brutality in the eyes of some VILLAGERS.

Unlike THE VILLAGE and other "black towns," there were all-white communities in the U.S. during the first half of the twentieth century whose residents perceived themselves as members of an open, nonoppressive, democratic society with which they closely identified.[36] This is not surprising. Nor is it surprising that similar rhetoric of praise and acclaim for the United States did not surface among Miles Heights VILLAGERS. African Americans of the VILLAGE had come to know firsthand a history of race-related social oppression and the intransigence of the colorline, factors contributing to their personal and social degradation, outcomes with which their white counterparts did not have to contend.

Some of Frog's popularity and respect among VILLAGERS, especially among young adults, came from his deviance from the customary ways in which blacks had learned to "git low" in response to whites in authoritative positions. As symbolized, in part, by VILLAGER support of Frog, and as interpreted by Blackwell,[37] racial and ethnic communities like THE VILLAGE are in part responses to outgroup prejudices, discrimination, segregation, and the accompanying experiences of opression.

> "Frog was a Miles Heights hero. To me, in my childhood, Frog was the first person who was not what we call a typical niggah. I mean, he would buck white authority, whereas all other times, if one white man would come to visit the neighborhood, that represented authority, everybody would buckle under. And all of a sudden one man [Frog] said,

'I'm not going to do that' and defied them. He took an ass whipping for it, but he did it. That is one thing that always stuck in my mind about Frog."[38]

It should be noted that Frog was not merely a physically tough character without humility. He was, indeed, a sensitive person who also expressed kindnesses that were not unknown to VILLAGERS. According to Nate Brooks, who grew up in THE VILLAGE and became bantamweight champion of the world in 1954:

"Frog was a nice person. He was a very good friend of mine. We used to go out together.... I never had to worry about anything when Frog was with me because I knew I had somebody gonna watch my back.... Frog was a better fellow than most people seemed to realize. Frog was a gentle brute, if I can use a phrase like that."[39]

Just as the stories of Frog's strength and courage seemed to make him super-human to many VILLAGERS, stories about the way in which he died were equally incredible.

"As I remember it, I think he was down there around the old A.C. Williams store, you know that section down there, and he was eating watermelon, greenapples, and drinking wine. They called the rescue squad to him, took him to the hospital and he never recovered. It [Frog's death] was related to the greenapples, but it could have been some other complications."[40]

It is worthy of note that Nate Brooks, the premier pugilist of THE VILLAGE was personally familiar with Frog and thought well of him. It is also noteworthy that each of the three folk heroes of THE VILLAGE were familiar with and respected each other, even though each clearly was involved with and respected individually among the masses of VILLAGERS for quite different reasons.

It should also be noted that while a history of race-related social oppression distinguished THE VILLAGERS from inhabitants of small white communities in the U.S. and induced some strain in their relations with white outsiders, the comraderie and equalitarian relations shown among the folk heroes and other people of THE VILLAGE showed the similarity of its internal social relations to those of other small towns. In their study of Springdale, New York, Vidich and Bensman refer to this phenomenon as "just plain folks."[41] To some extent, the term "folk" for Springdalers, like "Villager" for residents of old Miles Heights, distinguishes insiders from outsiders, but these terms also signify the essential oneness that VILLAGERS felt with each other; sharing each others joys and sorrows, successes and failures, regardless of education level, economic class, or differences in political power. More evidence of the close ties and equalitarian nature of relations among THE VILLAGERS will be seen in the pages that follow.

The Pugilist

A pugilist is a fighter or professional boxer. One of the distinctive features of THE VILLAGE, although not necessarily peculiar to it, was the importance assigned to the art of boxing between 1940 and 1960.

At least nine families among THE VILLAGE settlers who had arrived there by 1940 produced one or more Golden Glove and prizefighting contenders, some of whom went on to win titles through professional prizefighting. There were several incentives in THE VILLAGE and in the economy for becoming a prizefighter. Nate Brooks was the most successful pugilist of THE VILLAGE.

The Brooks family moved to THE VILLAGE in the late 1920s. Nate, born in 1933, was exposed to talk about sports and the importance of trying to be the best, whatever the event, from an early age. The elder Brooks was himself not a boxer, but he was a man who placed a high value on physical prowess and participation in sports activities.

> "My father was one of the gentlest people you'll ever meet and could be a very private man. [He] always encouraged me to fight and if you've ever been in the arena when I was performing and Dad was there, you'd know he was there. He liked sports. He liked fighting. He felt that men are supposed to show themselves and prizefighting was the way."[42]

In addition to incentives given by his father, Nate and the other aspiring young pugilists found encouragement from other VILLAGERS who recognized talent and knew the rewards that could come through a successful career of prizefighting.

> "Boxing was something that you grew up with. At that time, you're young and you're black. You have to do something, you know. And it was something that I started doing. Everybody was telling me from the very beginning how good I was which was heady music for a kid when you're 13 or 14 years old. Everybody telling you you're good. So you listen, you know. Your older brothers are doing the same thing. And you wind up, you're into something."[43]

As young adult males from poor families that had difficulties "making ends meet," economic rewards for success were another set of major incentives for many Afro-Americans to enter prizefighting. Jack Johnson and Joe Lewis had helped pave the way for blacks to enter this sport.

> Jack Johnson worked as a dockhand in his native Galveston [Texas] before he became a boxer at the turn of the Century. After a two year struggle to get a championship fight, Johnson knocked out Tommy Burns in Australia during 1908 to become Heavyweight Champion of the

World. He defeated several challengers including Middleweight Champion Stanley Ketchell in 1909 and former Heavyweight Champion Jim Jeffries in 1910. Johnson lost his title to Jess Willard in Havanna, Cuba, during 1915, but continued to box for several years. Ironically, the Texas legislature banned films of his victories over white boxers for fear they would cause Negro riots.[44]

The pervasiveness of economic poverty and the shortage of alternative ways of making a living for residents of THE VILLAGE did not end with the passing of the Great Depression. Unemployment was especially menacing to large families, such as the Brooks--a family of ll in the late 1930s with a single source of income.

Prizefighting was a potential way out of poverty for the few who had the courage, physical strength and stamina to withstand the challenges. According to Nate Brooks, the interest in prizefighting among blacks as a means of making a living had spread across the country by the end of the Depression.

> "It was very few things that a young black could get into. There was Joe Lewis, a role model. The only way they escaped this poverty was to become a fighter. That's why it was so hard to be a good fighter back then, because everybody was

fighting. You had to fight some hard fighters. They wouldn't fight to see who won, they'd fight to see who lived."[45]

Other avenues for economic mobility through professional sports came later, especially in the major leagues of baseball, basketball, and football. The forces for racial discrimination and segregation prevented access of blacks to those arenas until nearly a decade later.

"There was, you know, Larry Doby and these cats; Jackie Robinson--they came along after. Football, basketball, baseball, all this was a new thing. These things didn't exist then (in the 1930s and early 40s) for blacks. If you wanted to get away from this [poverty] then, you had to become a fighter."[46]

All eight of the Brooks boys went into the Golden Gloves. But their careers were not equally illustrious. Nate's was the most outstanding. Among his major victories were the International Golden Gloves Bantamweight Championship in 1951, the Olympics Flyweight Championship in 1952, and as a professional boxer, the North American Bantamweight Championship in 1954.

"I won the gloves in Cleveland three years in a row, 1949, 50, and 51. I won it in Chicago two years, 1950, 51. I won it in New York two years, 1950, 51. I won the International Golden Gloves Bantamweight Championship in 1951. I won the Ohio Gloves in Columbus in 1952, and won the Olympics Flyweight Division in 1952. Then, I turned pro and won the North American Bantamweight Championship in February, 1954."[47]

Brooks' reign as the North American Bantamweight Champion was an occasion for celebration, but short lived. By September, 1954, he had lost the title. Nevertheless, he continued to fight until his retirement from the ring in 1956. Since his retirement, Brooks has worked as a Surveyor for the Ohio State Department of Highways.

With respect to other folk heroes of **THE VILLAGE**, it is worthy of note that just as Nate Brooks was familiar with Frog, he also had a friendly relationship with Arthur R. Johnston.

"He was a very good friend. He was my buddy. He and I had a close relationship. It was the type of relationship that only two people could have who had been through this kind of stuff."[48]

In the closing statement of this quotation, Brooks is making reference to the fact that Johnston had been an amatuer pugilist himself long before Brooks' entry into the Golden Gloves. Johnston continued to be a fan of prizefighters until his death, especially the Brooks boys, who lived across the street from the Johnstons in THE VILLAGE.

Black Country Politician Makes Good

A detailed account of the life and times of Arthur R. Johnston is given in the next chapter. Here, however, attention is drawn briefly to his distinctive characteristics.

Johnston's status as a folk hero in THE VILLAGE already has been established. Equally noteworthy was his ability to succeed in politics in spite of his black identity and a 1929 campaign for the office of mayor in which he had to run against a white opponent in a predominantly white Miles Heights village. His victory marked one of the most distinguished achievements in the long history of African Americans in northeastern Ohio. In spite of his success, Johnston remained a man of considerable humility and a pillar of the black community.

CHAPTER 3

POWER AND POLITICS: ON ARTHUR R. JOHNSTON, FIRST BLACK MAYOR IN THE HISTORY OF CUYAHOGA COUNTY, OHIO

An inaugural ball in honor of Mayor Arthur R. Johnston of Miles Heights Village, the only Negro Mayor in Ohio, will be held Thursday, January 16 [1929], at Elks Hall, 2226 East 55th Street, under the auspices of the Miles Heights Chamber of Commerce (*Cleveland Plain Dealer*, 1929).[1]

"They always proclaimed he was the first black mayor. He was a politician. He was a good orator. And he knew his facts too. He studied a lot. He was recognized as one of the most respected persons to speak for blacks. He influenced a lot of whites too (James Gary, Jr., 1974)."[2]

Considering the social oppression of black Americans that was still pervasive in the United States during the early twentieth century, the predominantly white population of old Miles Heights in 1927, and the early twentieth century exclusion of blacks from top political offices, especially in predominantly white settlements within the United States, Arthur R. Johnston had a remarkably successful political career. His achievement of positions of political leadership in Miles Heights village, Cuyahoga County, and the State of Ohio are especially noteworthy. Included among Johnston's achievements were his election to the School Board of Miles Heights (1926), election to the Council of Miles Heights (1927), and his election to the Presidency of the Council of Miles Heights (1928).

The absence of large numbers of blacks who succeeded in winning elective offices in the State of Ohio from the end of the Civil War through the early twentieth century was not a matter of happenstance. Race discrimination, poll taxes, literacy tests and fear of punitive treatment by whites in response to the exercise of the franchise by blacks were key factors. Also key, as pointed out by Woodson,[3] was the relatively small population of blacks in the various localities of Ohio in contrast to their greater density in the southern states. These observations help to further establish the social and political significance of Johnston's election to public office.

This chapter focuses in particular on Johnston's succession to the office of Mayor of Miles Heights village and his administration of that office. His election established him as the first black mayor in the history of Cuyahoga County.[4]

Johnston was the incumbent president of the Miles Heights village Council in 1928 at the age of 36 years, and succeeded Mayor Dennis H. Von Benken in January, 1929. Von Benken died in office late in December 1928. Then in the Fall of 1929, Johnston won election to a full two-year term as mayor.[5] While it is probably true that Johnston's election campaign was not as strenuous as the challenge faced by Carl Stokes 38 years later in his campaign for election to the office of Mayor of Cleveland, Johnston's elections as president of village council in 1928 and as mayor in 1929 were no less notable.

Family Life

Arthur R. Johnston was born to Daniel and Susan Johnston in Southfield, Jamaica, British West Indies, September 5, 1892 (Parton, 1976; Fantroy, December 27, 1983).[6] The Johnstons of Jamaica were a poor family. However, through intelligence, hard work, and parents who had a strong need for achievement by their offspring, several of the Johnston children succeeded in getting training in nursing and medicine, and subsequently pursued successful careers in their respective fields of study.[7] This was indeed a family of high achievers.

Around 1905, when Arthur was 13 years of age, his parents moved with him from Southfield Jamaica to Battle Creek, Michigan. It is not clear whether other offspring or other family members moved with the Johnstons. Arthur was enrolled in Jackson High School in Battle Creek, where he received the diploma in 1909.[8]

In the Fall of 1909, Johnston was enrolled in the Medical Missionary College in Detroit, Michigan, where he remained for two years.[9] He was forced to discontinue his studies of medicine because of increasing economic pressures and declining resources of his parents. He then enrolled for studies of accounting at the School of Accountancy of the Young Mens Christian Association (YMCA) of Detroit. After completing this training for accounting, he moved to Cleveland, in 1913 looking for work.[10]

Shortly after moving to Cleveland, and after a three month courtship, Johnston married Annabell French, New Years Eve, 1913, at a private home in Cleveland, with the Reverend Horace C. Bailey, Pastor of Antioch Baptist Church officiating.[11] After the marriage, the Johnston's lived at 4116 Cedar Avenue, then moved to East Boulevard. To the couple two daughters were born: Constance, 1915, and Leola, 1916. Both still live in Cleveland.

In 1917, Johnston enlisted for military service in the United States Army. After two years, 1917-1919, he earned the rank of sergeant.[12] During his period of military service, Johnston also became a naturalized citizen of the United States on May 9, 1918.[13]

Following the completion of his tour of duty and return to his family in Cleveland, the Johnstons moved from East Boulevard to Orleans Avenue. Subsequently the family moved to East 126th Street in Cleveland, where they lived for a short time before moving to 147th Street in old Miles Heights late in the year 1919.[14]

In 1919, the Johnston home was a small, wood frame four room structure: 2 bedrooms, a kitchen and a living room heated by a coal burning stove. Laundry was done in the backyard, except in the winter months, when the kitchen was the major center of activity.[15] According to the late Mrs. Annabell Johnston:

> "My husband always told me that he'd make me an honest living and he did. He even carried garbage in East Cleveland when things got bad. After he became Mayor, [he] tried to rid the place of these joints (speakeasies) that moved in too."[16]

Even while ill, Johnston wanted to be useful, as he had been during his period as a public servant.

> He was sick for fifteen years. He used to always say, 'I don't want to be a burden on anybody.' He was sick all that time" [from around 1942 to 1957, when he died.[17]

The humility and commitment to being a useful person shown by Johnston in his family life pervaded his work as a public servant as well. Perhaps it was also his humility, honesty, and commitment to hard work that made him an attractive candidate to black and white voters during the elections of 1927 and 1929 to fill the top political offices of Miles Heights village.

Johnston's commitment to community service was reflected partly in his participation in church activities. He and his family were active members of the Antioch Baptist Church throughout their residence in Cleveland. Moreover, within THE VILLAGE, they participated in the Saint Paul Methodist Church during the early years of their residence; and subsequently the family became more active in the Canaan Missionary Baptist church. The surviving Johnston daughters were unable to account for the shift from the Saint Paul Methodist to the Canaan Baptist church.

The Rise of Miles Heights Village

Miles Heights village was incorporated in August, 1927, by the Cuyahoga County commissioners upon petition of the required number of property owners. The village then had a population of less than 1,500 people. The assessed valuation on real and personal property totalled only $5,663,600. At the first regular election in the fall of 1927, only 635 votes were cast from the two election precincts. This total was increased by only 200 votes in 1929.[18]

This quotation describes the legal, electoral and economic background that helped to form Miles Heights village. At a special election on August 16, 1927, Dennis H. Von Benken was chosen to be the first mayor of THE VILLAGE. At the same time, the first city clerk, treasurer, marshall and a Council of six members also were elected. Arthur R. Johnston was elected as the first president of THE VILLAGE Council in January, 1928.[19]

As noted earlier, Mayor Von Benken died in office in December, 1928. As a result, Johnston as President of Council, was appointed mayor to fill the vacancy. Subsequently, in the municipal election held in the Fall of 1929, Johnston was elected to serve a full two year term.[20]

THE VILLAGE 50

According to an account in the *Cleveland Plain Dealer*, March 29, 1932: "Johnston, a Negro, had led the Council ticket at the polls in the 1927 election." Another account of Johnston's vote getting abilities stated the following:

> Johnston ...was elected as representative of THE VILLAGE's large colored population and was made Council President last January (1928). He led all other Council candidates, getting more than 500 votes out of approximately 600 cast.[21]

While there is no doubt that Johnston's appeal to the voters helped to account for his election, it should be noted that his success also may be attributed in part to complacency and apathy among the estimated 600 white registered voters versus the 400 blacks. In addition, that the majority of blacks in THE VILLAGE were Republican and that the leaders of the Republican party of Cleveland and Cuyahoga County were looking for a candidate who could win helped considerably to achieve Johnston's success. According to the late James Gary, Jr., a personal chauffeur for Johnston during his 1927 and 1929 campaigns, the candidate was supported by the Republicans of Cleveland because of his vote getting ability.

> "He [Johnston] was backed for Council [in 1927] to get the votes down here [in THE VILLAGE]. In here [THE VILLAGE], the balance of power was in black hands. Blacks controlled it. Up

there [outside THE VILLAGE, but within the boundaries of old Miles Heights], there were just a few white Republicans, but a lot of Democrats. There were more black Republicans than white Democrats in Miles Heights; most of the black Republicans lived in THE VILLAGE. He could have been elected on the black vote alone. But some whites voted too."[22]

The suggestion that white voter complacency along with black and Republican bloc voting may have been major factors in Johnston's victories is consistent with recent findings of Watson in her study of the *Second Time Around* in black mayoral reelection campaigns.[23] She found that bloc voting by blacks occurred in 7 of 8 successful campaigns for election and re-election of black mayoral candidates in racially mixed cities in the United States between 1967 and 1982.[24] Johnston's success also suggests that, to some extent, the community leaders of old Miles Heights between 1927-29 had succeeded in resolving one of the major political problems of blacks since emancipation: acquiring and maintaining a critical mass; "a sufficient number of people for influencing political outcomes or decisions in regard to collective black interests."[25]

In Johnston's case, the attempt by the Cleveland and Cuyahoga County Republicans to influence his performances, and through him THE VILLAGE, continued after his election to office.

> "The Republicans dictated everything prior to Von Benken's death. Johnston was President of Council, you know. Everything was dictated by Bud Allen; at that time he was head custodian in Cleveland City Hall and Chief Highway Inspector.... Practically everything was strictly Republican out here."[26]

This statement anticipates Blauner's[27] description of community outsiders who attempt to manipulate insider behavior under "domestic colonialism." To some extent, however, political party attempts to manipulate performances of newly elected officers is a general outcome of the exercise of political power.

After his succession to the mayor's office, Johnston appointed two black residents of THE VILLAGE to key posts in his administration: William Simmons as Building Inspector, a cabinet level position, and Mark Anthony as one of the four police officers in THE VILLAGE.[28] Mark Anthony was the son of Jewell Anthony, head of one of the oldest black families that settled in THE VILLAGE in 1918. William Simmons was married to one of the offspring of the family of Jewell Anthony. Plate Number 3.1 shows Johnston, key members of his staff, and the members of the Council of Miles Heights in 1929, including William Simmons and Mark Anthony.

Johnston apparently had won the respect of large numbers of whites and blacks in the predominantly white Miles Heights village and had the support of several village interest

Plate Number 3.1
Arthur R. Johnston (seated at the center of the table) and the Council of Miles Heights village, 1929

Standing, Top Row: (L to R) Sam Provateir (Policeman), Tom Glassburner (Chief of Police), Unknown, Alfred Eiden (Custodian), William Simmons (Building Inspector), Mark Anthony (Policeman), Tony Miklaus (Policeman)

It should be noted that the Council members standing in the second row, and to the left and right of A.R. Johnston could not be identified by the informants for this study.

Source of the photograph: Constance Parton, Oldest surviving daughter of Arthur R. Johnston, June, 1982.

groups who supported him in 1930 to run for election to a second term as mayor. However, he chose not to run because of his dismay about the scandal ridden behavior of other elected and appointed officials of Miles Heights who had gained public attention during his term as Mayor. Perhaps this problem and Johnson's dismay were partly a reflection of Blackwell's and Haug's[29] observation that gaining control of a mayoralty by blacks does not necessarily mean significant social and political rewards. The following excerpt from a 1931 issue of the *Cleveland Plain Dealer* helps to reveal Johnston's feelings in response to his nomination for a second term as mayor:

> Mayor A. R. Johnston of Miles Heights village last night announced that he would not be a candidate for mayor again. Only Negro chief executive in Cuyahoga County's family of municipalities, Johnston is serving his second term. 'I'm just tired,' Johnston explained, 'You know I didn't want to run the second time. I never saw the petition that nominated me then. I think I'll get a farm and a pair of horses and forget all this. I reckon I'm not enough of a politician.'[30]

According to Mrs. Annabell Johnston, the late wife of the former mayor: "I never wanted him to go into politics because I knew an honest upright person cannot thrive in politics."[31] While corruption might have been a major reason for Johnston's decision not to seek a second term, there were many other circumstances that helped to account for the decline of THE VILLAGE and its subsequent annexation by the City of Cleveland.

Between 1915 and 1929, numerous public discussions among the people of the Cleveland metropolitan district debated whether or not Greater Cleveland should have one metropolitan government or continue to have dozens of local governments.[32] In 1927, with the incorporation of Miles Heights Village, its presence drew the negative attention of the opponents of local governments just as other small governments, such as Warrensville, Parma, Garfield and others had done before Miles Heights. The investigative reporting initiated by the Citizens League of Cleveland in 1930, focusing on the "ills of suburban separateness," in which Miles Heights village was treated as typical of all of the local villages, spawned a series of analyses critical of various features of Miles Heights that documented its problems and made a case for annexation. Included in this criticism were deficit spending, inability to meet the payroll of public school teachers and other employees, the risk of closing the schools and thus failing to meet the public mandate to provide a basic education and poor public sanitation facilities. The growing sentiments of Miles Heights residents to vote for annexation to solve internal problems led to the eventual annexation and with it the end of the short five (5) year existence of Miles Heights village.

The Nemeses of Old Miles Heights

Abuses of Power and Uses of Public Funds for Personal Gain

The governmental requirements of old Miles Heights were modest from its incorporation in 1927. The salary of the mayor was $75.00 per month, too little to sustain Johnston and his family. To help compensate for this, Mayor Johnston also held a job as a foreman of sewer inspection with the Cuyahoga County Sanitary Department.

The offices for the elected officials and other employees of Miles Heights village were located in rented former storerooms at the intersection of Lee Road and Miles Avenue, the central business district of old Miles Heights throughout its period of incorporation.[33] In the same vicinity was the Miles Heights schoolhouse, Beehive School, a modest but modern building.

A large proportion of the streets were unpaved, without sanitary sewers and ample sources of water for residents.[34] The growing number of small resident-owned homes contributed to Miles Height's tax valuation of $4,288,000.[35]

In spite of this modest beginning, "a politics-ridden administration began a tax spending orgy shortly after incorporation that ran the tax rate up from $1.96 for 1927 to $2.38 for the year 1931."[36] Along with the excessive spending of the local government, the general economic downturn in the United States brought by "The Great Depression" resulted in unemployment for many taxpayers, which exacerbated the increasing gap between the spending level and available revenue of old Miles Heights.[37] The inability of the Miles Heights school district to pay the salaries of teachers and custodians for the full academic year 1930-31 and to afford to open the schools in the Fall of 1931 helps to illustrate the depths of the financial disaster.

The exposure of abuses of power first occurred when the state examiner uncovered mismanagement of service contracts issued by old Miles Heights in 1929 which penalized property owners with excessive engineering and legal fees for street improvements.[38] Moreover,

> ...The Miles Heights payroll was being stretched to accommodate relatives of village officials. The wives of both The Miles Heights clerk and the treasurer were hired to assist them in their duties, after which the clerk of an adjacent village was hired to do much of the work which the two men and their wives were already being paid for.[39]

As criticism mounted and Miles Heights was singled out as an "example of what a suburban government should not be," the sentiments for annexation also grew.[40] The financial problems of the Miles Heights Board of Education, of which Mayor Arthur R. Johnston had been a member, only made matters worse.

The Struggle to Save Beehive School

Beehive School was founded in Warrensville Township Cuyahoga County, Ohio in 1916. According to a former principal of the school who is the daughter of an early settler of THE VILLAGE, the school was named after a local farm whose owner specialized in growing and harvesting the products of honey bees.[41]

Before incorporation of Miles Heights in 1927, the school district as well as the residential subdivision that became Miles Heights were under the auspices of the commissioners of Warrensville Township.[42] Upon incorporation of Miles Heights, the school district was included within the boundaries of THE VILLAGE and the school was renamed Miles Heights Elementary and High School. By this procedure, the boundaries of Miles Heights became coterminous with those of the Beehive School district (see chapter 2, plate no. 2.1, for the street boundaries of old Miles Heights). It should be noted that village residents continued to refer to the school as "Beehive" in spite of the incorporation of Miles Heights and the renaming of the school.[43]

While school activities got off to a good start in 1927 under the newly incorporated Miles Heights village, several problems had developed by 1930 that threatened to undermine the school and the stability of Miles Heights itself. For example, on September 23, 1931 it was reported that five teachers had resigned in the Miles Heights school district because of the inability of the school board to pay the teachers back wages from the previous school year, 1930-31. Moreover, the school with its 700 students was financially unable to open in September of 1931 and there was widespread public concern that the school might not open at all.[44] Several events led to this financial and educational crisis. Among them were delinquent tax receipts.

Owners of property in old Miles Heights who failed to pay their taxes on time contributed to an $80,000 tax deficit in 1931. The delinquent tax payers were major contributors to the inability of the school board and the Miles Heights village Council to meet their respective financial obligations, including the salaries of teachers, coal for the heating plant and supplies for the school.[45]

Various efforts were undertaken to keep "Beehive" open. In early October, 1931, members of the primarily white Parent-Teacher Association (PTA) showed their concern through efforts to collect used books by a house-to-house canvass.[46] In addition, about 50 of the PTA members stated their willingness to contribute $2.00 each to help reopen the school. While no collection was attempted at that time, members of the PTA did pledge to carry on fundraising efforts to help get the school reopened.[47] It should be noted by modern day readers that $2.00 per PTA member may seem like a small amount of money in terms of 1986 dollars. But in 1931, it represented a sizeable contribution, about 4 percent of the monthly salaries of some persons.[48] Moreover, the support shown by the PTA was consistent with the general spirit of togetherness and mutually supportive relations that characterized villagers in many other activities, such as donations of volunteer construction labor in building the Saint Paul Methodist Church and homes for new residents, as well as other areas of mutual interest among Miles

Heights villagers. It should be noted also that there was one integrated PTA, not a black and a white one, in spite of the patterns and sanctions during this period for racial separatism in public accommodatons elsewhere in the United States.

The public school system and Parent Teachers Association of old Miles Heights were racially integrated throughout the period from 1917 to 1980, when the Beehive School closed. Although whites were in the majority, outnumbering Afro-Americans by three to one, there were no formal attempts to exclude blacks from access to public accommodations nor from participation in determining policy and managing the affairs of old Miles Heights.

In August, 1931, the Board of Education borrowed $15,000 from the Ohio Teachers Pension Fund to pay off all except one month of the back salaries of the teachers and custodians of the school that were due in honor of contracts issued for the previous school year, 1930-31. Then, in September, 1931, the Board voted 4-to-1 to petition the tax commissioner of Ohio for permission to issue tax delinquency bonds equal to $26,900 under provisions of the Hyre Act.[49] The Hyre Act provided that school districts in which taxes are 33 1/3 percent delinquent may issue bonds to 80 percent of the delinquency. It was the intention of the Board to use the revenue raised by the bonds to pay off the $15,000 debt to the Teachers Pension Fund and open the school for the 1931-32 academic year. However, the Board found no relief through this approach. On October 2, 1931, an article appeared in the *Cleveland Plain Dealer* reporting that the Board's petition had been rejected by the State Auditor, Joseph T. Tracey.[50] Following the Auditor's decision, the

Board of Education decided by a tie vote to keep the school closed to its 700 students.[51]

The school remained closed until December 17, 1931, when a court order forced the Board to resume classes.[52] The leadership of two members of the school Board and a member of the Village Council, coupled with the dismay of many village residents over the uncertainty of educational opportunities for their children induced a growing proportion of councilmen and villagers to favor annexation. Unhealthy environmental conditions in old Miles Heights only helped to make matters worse.

Environmental Health Hazards

The failure and/or inability of the Miles Heights government to provide a sanitary environment for its residents was one of the major arguments against maintaining it as a district separate from the City of Cleveland. The results of a health survey of THE VILLAGE published in 1932 revealed that less than 50 percent of the households and streets had sanitary conveniences.[53] For example, one observation revealed a street "where refuse flows into open sewer ditches on each side of the street."[54]

Furthermore, the health survey showed the following:

> Only a few streets have the sanitary facilities that are demanded in Cleveland by the health ordinance. Drainage conditions are bad in several parts of Miles Heights. This means that a typhoid

> hazard exists and in some respects it will be an advantage to have the suburb annexed. For if a typhoid epidemic breaks out, it knows no political boundary lines. We shall now (with annexation) be in a position to correct conditions and to combat any epidemic there.[55]

The survey conducted by the office of the Cleveland City Health Commissioner after the City Council voted for annexation clearly showed that containment of a health hazard within Miles Heights that was near epidemic proportions was one of the major incentives for annexation. Improvement of procedures for sewage disposal would provide mutual benefits: both the people of old Miles Heights and those of Cleveland would secure preventive health care and a higher quality of life.

Annexation of Miles Heights to the City of Cleveland

Following a vote for annexation by a majority of the residents and the Council of Miles Heights in the Fall of 1931, it was just a matter of political maneuvering and time before the linkages were complete. It should be noted that, according to the late James Gary, Jr., an early settler, black registered voters in Miles Heights were more numerous than their white counterparts, and more in favor of annexation.

> A lot of white folks didn't want to go. Of we [blacks] down here [in THE VIL-

LAGE], most did. But the few whites, they wasn't particular about annexing this. It never was publicized much because the Republicans had control of the 15th ward that adjoins the Miles Heights area. The Republicans influenced bringing Miles Heights into the City of Cleveland."[56]

In terms of electoral clout, as they succeeded in placing A.R. Johnston in office as a Council member in 1927 and Mayor in 1929, blacks in THE VILLAGE also had the votes for annexation over white voter opposition in 1931.

On March 28, 1932, the City Council of Cleveland voted, 20 to 3, to approve annexation of Miles Heights village.[57] With the signature of the Mayor of Cleveland, the ordinance took effect 40 days after March 28.

Since the Cleveland and the Miles Heights Boards of Education were politically separate from their respective city and village governments, each would have to act autonomously to bring about annexation of the school districts. The proper actions were taken and the Miles Heights school district was annexed to the Cleveland district late in the Spring of 1932.[58] These events helped to mark the end of the incorporated village of Miles Heights and the Miles Heights school district, but not the end of the achievements of A.R. Johnston.

THE VILLAGE 64

Other Milestones in Johnston's Career

Following the end of his term as mayor and the annexation of old Miles Heights, Johnston was appointed Director of Purchases for the City of Cleveland.[59] He remained in this position from 1932 through 1938.

On October 16, 1939, Johnston was appointed Tax Examiner in the Ohio Department of Taxation by Governor John Bricker. Although this was a provisional appointment, it marked the first time in the history of the State of Ohio that a black person was appointed to this position.[60] Moreover, this appointment established Johnston as the only black appointee in the Department of Taxation, a branch of the State government in 1939. Subsequently, Johnston was given a permanent appointment as Tax Examiner, which office he retained until he was forced to retire at the age of 63 in 1955. By that time he had developed Parkinson's disease and become too ill to carry on his work.

At 65 years of age, Arthur R. Johnston died in Cleveland City Hospital on Wednesday, April 23, 1957. He was buried in the Highland Park Cemetery with the Reverend Wade Hampton McKinney, Antioch Baptist Church officiating, the same institution through which he and his wife Annabell were married 44 years earlier.[61]

Conclusions

While the death of Johnston was an occasion for mourning in the family and the community alike, the kind of community solidarity that contributed to his successful career as a politician continues among THE VILLAGERS, although larger numbers are Democrats now than was the case during the late 1920s. In spite of the difficulties encountered by Johnston, the short length of his mayoralty, and the annexation of old Miles Heights to the City of Cleveland, winning election to the Office of Mayor in a predominantly white political district was noteworthy.

In the next three Chapters, features of health care, church, and economic life in THE VILLAGE will be examined. Some of the public health problems that contributed to public criticism of the Miles Heights government during the Johnston mayoralty and raised questions about the competency of its administration are discussed in further detail in the next chapter, "Health, Illness, and Coping with Adversity." In addition, the next chapter will show the intricate linkages between family organization and health care practices in the everyday life of THE VILLAGE.

CHAPTER 4

HEALTH, ILLNESS, AND COPING WITH ADVERSITY

"Basically, the health care system in Miles Heights was poor. A lot of us were born by midwives. Available to us at that time was the City Hospital. That was located on the West Side, on Scranton Road. At that time there was virtually no welfare stuff, but there were some free health services. You had to go down on 35th and Woodland. By bus, it was a two hour ride from THE VILLAGE. If anybody had an emergency they would be in trouble."(Johnell Gresham)[1]

•••••••••••

"When you got a doctor, it be the last minute. Susan had the pneumonia once and I was doing all I could do for her. Other folks tell me things to do and I kept a doing. But she wasn't getting no better. I told Scott to go get the doctor. He had to go a ways outside THE VILLAGE. The doctor gave her one little pink pill and a teaspoon of water. And she got better." (Mary Lou Watson).[2]

Like every individual and organized group, residents of THE VILLAGE developed ways of coping with illness in everyday life. The combination, however, of the nearest hospital located several miles away, poverty, and poor public transportation made professional services scarce.

Until 1954, when the Marymont Hospital was completed in Garfield Heights (1 & 1/2) miles away), the nearest general hospitals to THE VILLAGE were the old Cleveland Charity Hospital (18 miles away) and the Highland View Hospital (16 miles away). For serious injuries and acute illnesses that could not be treated at home, VILLAGERS were in jeopardy. However, the people were not cut off from all health care outside THE VILLAGE.

> "It wasn't like health care was totally lacking. It was like just the regular stuff, like if you got scarlet fever, you would have to go through some changes to get help somewhere. But if you got cut or something, I can remember ambulances coming out there to pick up the hurt."[3]

Sanitation

In addition to the absence of nearby hospitals and clinics, poor public health facilities exacerbated problems in the prevention of illness among VILLAGERS. Outhouses and open sewage ditches were especially menacing until the late 1940s.

THE VILLAGE

Outhouses

The outhouse was a small shed designed for use during the elimination of human bodily wastes. This kind of facility, depicted on Plate Number 4.1 was usually a detached wood frame building, with one or more stools situated over earthen pots which fit into holes made by the excavation of the land to form concave structures to catch and contain deposits of human wastes until the monthly cleaning and burning occurred. Cleaning of outhouses was a problem believed to have the possibility of causing disease and pestilence in THE VILLAGE.

The "honey dipper" was a folk term used to refer to an itinerant worker whose job was to collect and dispose of wastes deposited in outhouses. The term comes from the long spoon-like ladle used to reach into the pit(s) that formed the earthen pot or toilet inside each outhouse. Once the waste was collected in a closeable container, it was hauled away to a county dump where it was destroyed by burning. On any given day of cleaning, the pungent foul odor that filled the air let everyone know that the honey dipper was making his rounds. The problem with this cleaning process, like modern day garbage collections and other kinds of waste dumps, was the leakage that often occurred, or that was claimed to have occurred, always raising the spectre of whether or not the process of cleaning and dumping itself as well as the outhouse was a health hazard.

Plate 4.1

An outhouse that could be observed in THE VILLAGE from the date of the early settlers through the 1950s. Sketch by John McKenzie, Stein Printing Company, 1988.

THE VILLAGE 70

Open sewage ditches

The problem of eliminating the wastes of outhouses by the use of county waste dumps was closely associated with the use of open sewage ditches that ran alongside most streets in THE VILLAGE carrying sewage from homes. While some home owners began to install (or have installed) systems of piped-in running water as early as the mid-1930s following annexation of THE VILLAGE to the City of Cleveland, it was not until the late 1940s that Cleveland extended underground storm and drainage systems to remove sewage from homes in THE VILLAGE. Plate number 4.2 depicts a street in THE VILLAGE with open sewage ditches that remained that way from the early 1920s through the decade of the 1940s. As seen in Chapter 3, these health hazards were among the poor living conditions that brought public protest and contributed to the pressures among VILLAGE residents for the annexation of old Miles Heights to the City of Cleveland in 1932. It was believed that annexation would bring an influx of new money and improvements in the quality of life in THE VILLAGE.

Doctors and Midwives

In spite of the absence of easily accessible hospitals and clinics and the inhospitable public health conditions, THE VILLAGERS multiplied and survived in growing numbers. Families ranging in size from 6 to 14 members were common. Country doctors who lived outside but made home visits in THE VILLAGE helped meet the needs for health care.

Plate 4.2

This plate shows a street scene in THE VILLAGE during the 1930s. As described in the *Cleveland Plain Dealer*, the streets of THE VILLAGE had no storm sewers, sidewalks, or pavements from its early years through the late 1940s when postwar housing developments in the area induced street improvements. When there was heavy rain, before the street improvements, the roads were at times impassable.

"Although there were no hospitals nearby before 1954, there were doctors. At that time, doctors would make house calls."[4]

"There were traveling country doctors in the South, even white doctors, just as there were in old Miles Heights. I did not notice any racial discrimination by doctors in the 1920s. It actually seems worse now than it was then."[5]

Even though some doctors lived near THE VILLAGE and were willing to make home visits, transportation problems caused by unmarked, unlit, and unpaved roads that were impassible in inclement weather made the delivery of medical services difficult. The following quote from an old-timer illustrates the problem.

"I remember the birth of one of my sons. It was snowing so bad that night. Oh, about 11:30 or 12 o'clock midnight. And shoutin, 'go git the docta, go git the docta, 'and here I done called the old bloomin doctor by Osborn Road to come out to the house. And it was snowing so bad he could hardly find the way. I met him on Osborn Road over there, had a little model T (Ford), and he was shining a flashlight--snowing so bad--he could hardly see. Said, 'good doctor, you goin to my house.' He said, 'yeh!' I said, 'follow me.' We got there and my son was there for a long time" [born, before we returned].[6]

When the Elie family completed the construction of its complex of general stores on Ohio Avenue in 1948, the first office for a medical doctor was established in THE VILLAGE. With the influx of newcomers into the new public housing projects completed toward the end of World War II, residents in THE VILLAGE swelled to numbers large enough to support a medical practice, a pharmacist and a drug store.

While access to health care institutions, country doctors, and other facilities were often impeded by distance, lack of personal and/or public transportation, and costs, VILLAGERS were not without alternative means of responding to illness and meeting their needs for health care.

> "Most of my chidlren were born at home. We had midwives. We didn't have money for a doctor to pay doctor's bills. Later in the 30s, we were on relief then, they would send a free doctor."[7]

The significance of midwives is also indicated by the son of another early settler who reported that all of the eight children in his family of origin were born by the hands of midwives.[8] Another important feature of self-help networks in THE VILLAGE was the presence of folk medical specialists in various families and/or neighborhoods.

"Mrs. Chapel was our [folk] medical director. She was our second aunt. It was common practice back in those times that if you had a lot of kids, you would take your kids and give them to a relative to raise if you couldn't afford to do it. So, my parents had me [Johnell], Zel, and Quench. Miss Chapel raised Quench because they could more afford to raise Quench than Bea and my father could. Quench got sick one time and had this high fever and he couldn't breathe. Called a doctor and the doctor said, 'heh, can't do no more. Kid gonna die.' Miss Chapel said, 'give me that boy.' Bea said she gave Miss Chapel a 'hot baby.' Miss Chapel took that boy home and she said 'Miss Chapel put a lot of polstices around him. Poured some castor oil in him, broke that fever in that boy.' See what we got; he didn't die."[9]

Another example:

"You know what my mother and them done to me. I hurt my leg, I never will forget it, we were playing baseball up there in front of Mr. Davis' house. I hurt my leg. They didn't take me to no doctor. You know what my mother and em done, they went out in the woods and got some black dirt and mixed it with something, and wrapped that crap around my leg and do you know that two days later that swelling had went down. One of them home remedies."[10]

Death in THE VILLAGE and Social Support for the Bereaved

Not only did VILLAGERS have to be innovative in meeting their health care needs to sustain the vitality of the living; they sometimes had to be equally innovative in helping to provide last rites for those whose "tickets had been taken" by the grand reaper. Once again, transportation in and out of THE VILLAGE during the winter months was especially difficult.

> "My father told me that when he first moved to Miles Heights (1922), the roads were so bad in the winter time that when somebody died, Spot Gray had a sled, he took the body on that sled up what we call Seville Road now, it was Mitchell Road then. It came up to Lee Road and Wills Hurst would be up there and give Spot $2.00 or $3.00 for bringing the body up there. It was that bad."[11]

There were yet other obstacles faced in securing proper treatment for the remains of the deceased, not the least of which were the hardships of the poor in affording a "decent burial."

THE VILLAGE

In most societies, death is a communal as well as a family affair.[12] Unaffordable burial costs, however, which often occur among the poor are especially likely to induce the need for communal economic support to buttress the meagre resources of the bereaved family.

The growing rate of unemployment and poverty in old Miles Heights that came with the Great Depression meant that many families did not own burial insurance policies nor have private means to pay the cost of funerals upon the death of family members. To compensate for the shortage of dollars and to express the essential togetherness that the community felt with the bereaved, VILLAGERs institutionalized the practice of making donations for the right of access to the potter's field. An old-timer describes this practice as follows:

> "A well known and trusted member of THE VILLAGE, usually someone close to the bereaved, would knock on doors, house to house and ask (or "beg," as one old timer phrased it) for money to help pay the cost of a proper burial for the deceased."[13]

Other than economic necessity, the proverbial "mother of invention," no one seemed to know the origin of the custom of begging for the deceased poor in THE VILLAGE. Since the majority of the early settlers had migrated to THE VILLAGE from small settlements in the southeastern United States, it was assumed that this custom, like others, might have been diffused from their settlements of origin. None of the oral historical interviews, however, nor other documents clearly corroborated this hunch.

In some instances, although rarely reported in this study, "passing the basket" in a local church to collect donations on behalf of the family of the bereaved was another means of helping them.[14] The preconditions and act of passing the basket were described as follows:

> "A member of the family, a close friend, or a close confidant of the bereaved, who could be the pastor or another member of the church, must bring the problem of poverty to the attention of the church. The family of the bereaved must be unable to pay the full costs of the funeral. The pastor will then offer prayer and ask the congregation for an offering for the bereaved family."[15]

In some instances in which the poor were unable to pay the full costs, the funeral director would permit the bereaved family to meet the costs by an initial down payment, and then to pay the balance in installments.[16] For this arrangement, however, the head of the family had to be creditable. No instances were reported in which a funeral director engaged in barter, such as accepting livestock or other non-cash media from the bereaved in exchange for funeral services.

Few among the poor families in THE VILLAGE carried life and/or burial insurance policies sufficient in cash surrender value to meet the full costs of a funeral, except for the most ordinary ceremony that might culminate in a potter's field. One old-timer commented this way:

> "That's the kind of insurance Ma had, the hundred dollar ... burial benefit. That's barely enough money to rent a funeral car now (in 1985). But, a hundred dollars was a lot of money for a funeral 50 years ago."[17]

In addition to the extremely small face value of many policies, the level of poverty is suggested further by the very small premiums payable for these policies. Ten cents ($.10) per week was the premium collected for whole life policies with a face value of $100.

These kinds of insurance policies and premiums reflect the precarious economic circumstances of poor blacks of the United States in the late nineteenth and the early twentieth centuries. Early black insurance companies such as the Union Central Relief Association of Alabama and the Atlanta Life Insurance Company of Georgia suffered from a very high turnover in membership because of non-payment of premiums, even though they were scaled down to meet the consumer's ability to pay, on the one hand, and to provide a death benefit at least sufficient to pay burial costs, on the other.[18] "Premiums ranged from 5 cents per week with a ten dollar death benefit and a one dollar per week sick benefit to a premium of 40 cents per week with an 80 dollar death benefit and 8 dollars per week sick benefit."[19]

Like the acquisition of many other commodities, the purchase of life insurance policies with large death benefits is closely tied to income of the consumers and their time orientation. Within time orientations, distinctions can be made among preoccupations with events past, present or futuristic. Assuming adequate capital, the purchase of life and/or burial insurance policies probably increases with the sense of mortality, a future time orientation, concern about the kind of burial ceremony that one may want for oneself, and the financial well being that the insured may wish for his or her prospective survivors. As one old-timer stated, "...most people don't be thinking about the costs of death and dying."[20]

Conclusions

Health care in THE VILLAGE was a challenge met through a variety of means. Although not easily accessible, hospital care that was available in Cleveland proper helped to provide needed health services. But in everyday life, home remedies and home visiting country doctors were the major sources of health care. Similar to the self-help intervention techniques that VILLAGERS developed to treat minor illnesses, they also came to each others aid, including the poor, to make decent burials available. The emphasis on self-help and mutual support was as pervasive in family life and health care as it was in the church.

Chapter 5

WADE IN THE WATER

The Negro church is the peculiar and characteristic product of the transplanted African, and deserves especial study. As a social group the Negro church may be said to have antedated the Negro family on American soil; as such it has preserved, on the one hand, many functions of tribal organization, and on the other hand, many of the family functions. Its tribal functions are shown in its religious activity, its social authority and general guiding and coordinating work; its family functions are shown by the fact that the church is a center of social life and intercourse;...indeed, the church is the world in which the Negro moves and acts. So far-reaching are these functions of the church that its organization is almost political (DuBois, 1899).[1]

Throughout the history of blacks in America and the social organization of their communities, religious beliefs and practices have been essential features of everyday life. This was as true of blacks in THE VILLAGE as it was of other small black communities in the history of the United States.[2]

As has already been shown, the earliest settlers of THE VILLAGE began to move into the area that came to be known as old Miles Heights around 1913. Along with family settlement came the religious beliefs and practices shared among the families and their kinship groups.

According to several old-timers with whom oral historical interviews were conducted, the first settlers in the area were of the Protestant and Catholic religions.[3] Among the early Afro-American settlers, two church groups, which represented two major denominations were formed: (1) Canaan Missionary Baptist Church, 1919,[4] and (2) Saint Paul Methodist Church, 1921.[5] All of the early Catholics were white and, in most instances, went to St. Timothies, the parish church in Cranwood Village, outside old Miles Heights. While a variety of other churches have been formed and settled in THE VILLAGE since 1919, only the Canaan and Saint Paul groups have survived since the appearance of the first settlers.

Canaan Missionary Baptist Church

The Canaan Missionary Baptist Church was the first group to organize for worship in THE VILLAGE. Under the leadership of its founding pastor, the Reverend Jordan, Canaan sprang from the spiritual soil of the people in 1919. The following account reports the founding of the church:

> In 1919, Mr. Sheets, a realtor, made a commitment with the Baptist and Methodist affiliated members of the

Miles Heights area that the denomination with the most members be given the corner lot which is now the present site of Canaan Missionary Baptist Church. The Baptist denomination with a membership of approximately fifty (50) members won the proposition. The late Reverend Jordan was the founder and first pastor of the church in the year 1921.[6]

The first home of the Canaan Baptists, built at the corner of Ohio Avenue and East 147th Street in old Miles Heights, was a small wood frame one room structure heated by a pot belly wood and coal burning stove.[7] As the church grew and expanded in membership, a cornerstone was laid in 1925 and can still be seen on the building at the original site.[8]

Following the initial efforts of the Reverend Jordan, the late Reverend E. M. Moore assumed the pastorate of the church for a ten (10)-year period, 1925-1934. Under the leadership of the Reverend Moore, the church engaged in a massive rebuilding program.[9] The entire physical plant was enlarged during this period and a new parsonage was constructed at 14705 Ohio Avenue, next door to the house of worship for the congregation.

Reverend Moore was succeeded by a Reverend Murray in 1935. Under the pastorate of Reverend Murray between 1935 and 1946, a schism emerged in the church:

The Trustees had a falling out with Reverend Murray. Some members went to the law and had him locked out [of the church].... The Trustees and the Reverend did not agree on a lot of things. Reverend Murray wanted all of the money to come through his hands and wanted his wife to be treasurer. He wanted to control everything. The Trustees disagreed. They thought the Trustees should handle the money and have some say about how it is spent. When Reverend Murray was locked out, some members left with him and formed the New Home Baptist Church.[10]

The New Home Baptist Church was organized in 1947 and located its house of worship at the corner of Sunview Avenue and East 153rd Street within THE VILLAGE.[11] The Saint Paul Methodist Church, the second oldest church in THE VILLAGE, then located on Naples Avenue near the corner of East 151st Street, took in some of the members who left Canaan.[12] The development of the Saint Paul Methodist Church is described in the next section of this chapter.

With the disintegration of the congregation of Canaan in 1946 and the departure of the Reverend Murray, the church was in need of new unifying leadership. The Reverend Wilbert J. Jackson, the sixth and current pastor of Canaan, came in 1947 and accepted the challenge of its leadership.[13] From 1947 to 1969 the congregation expanded rapidly from 100 to 700 members. In 1953, the church building was remodeled once again. This time a brick veneer was added over its wood frame, while improvements were made in the interior. By 1957, the church mortgage was paid in full.[14]

The continued growth of THE VILLAGE population and the congregation of Canaan required the church once more to expand and remodel its facility in 1965. But this was not the end of its growth and development. By 1978, the church membership had expanded to such an extent that it was necessary that the church move to a new site. After much deliberation, a decision was made to purchase the building that formerly housed the Clara Tag Brewer Elementary School at 4688 East 162nd Street, located just outside the southeastern border of the original VILLAGE. While many Canaan old-timers objected to this move, and some gave up their membership, the church has continued to thrive partly through attracting new members from its new community setting.

Saint Paul Methodist Church, 1921-1953

Like the founder(s) of the Canaan Missionary Baptist Church, St. Paul Methodist Church also grew out of the initiatives of early settlers of THE VILLAGE. In fact, according to Ferguson's "History of the Saint Paul Methodist Church," Mrs. Edna Lee--its founder in 1921--may have been a resident of THE VILLAGE settlement of old Miles Heights before World War I.[15] The conjecture about the actual date of the Lees' settlement stems from the writing of Ferguson who simply states that Mrs. Edna Lee"...had been in Cleveland a number of years before World War I," but does not explicitly state that the sub-area of Cleveland was THE

VILLAGE settlement in old Miles Heights.[16] However, Ferguson later implies that he indeed, may have had THE VILLAGE in mind (although his writing was not concise) when he stated that "Mrs. Lee, her husband, Henry, and her young son, Walter, were residents of this growing community and had established their home on Ohio Avenue."[17] The designation of Ohio Avenue, one of the major arteries of THE VILLAGE, as the place of the Lees' established residence, suggests the conclusion that the Lees may have been among pre-World War I settlers of THE VILLAGE.

While the special focus of this chapter is on the religious activities of blacks in THE VILLAGE, several Italian families were included among the early settlers and participants in the activities of the Sunday School that eventually developed into the Saint Paul Methodist Church. According to Ferguson:

> ...The people of the community in 1921 were predominantly of Italian decent. As a result, the original Sunday School was a mixed school of Negro and Italian children.[18]

Not all of the Italians in THE VILLAGE attended the churches organized by blacks. Some attended the services of Catholic churches that were nearby in Cranwood or Garfield Heights, Ohio, outside THE VILLAGE.[19] Although these notes are of interest as indicators of the integration of blacks and whites in the organization of church activities, no additional sources of information were available on racially mixed congregations of the early churches in THE VILLAGE.

THE VILLAGE

Early History

The Saint Paul Methodist Church had its origin in a Sunday School organized by Edna Lee, who saw the need in 1921 for improvements in the religious life of VILLAGE residents. In that year, the Sunday School was organized in her home on Ohio Avenue with the assistance of Mr. and Mrs. William Simmons, Mr. and Mrs. John Scott, and Mrs. Lee's husband, Henry Lee.[20] According to Ferguson's history, these same persons subsequently became the founding members of the church.[21]

Before formally organizing as the Saint Paul Methodist Church, the founders and the growing congregation relocated their place of worship twice between 1921 and 1924. After outgrowing the Lee's home, the church rented and moved to a larger home on Lawndale Avenue in THE VILLAGE.[22] However, because of the competition for rental space in THE VILLAGE and the inability of the Saint Paul congregation to compete with higher bidders, the group eventually had to vacate this property on Lawndale Avenue and seek a new church home.

This forced departure from the Lawndale site caused the church leaders to ponder a more permanent solution, leading to the purchase of a plot of land on the South side of Naples Avenue, just west of East 151st Street near the center of THE VILLAGE. This lot was purchased in the name of the trustees of the Saint Paul Methodist Church on February 13, 1923. Materials for the church were purchased from the Forest City Lumber Company and the construction labor was donated by members and friends. The original building that was erected without a basement measured approximately 28' x 24' in total floor area and seated about 30 persons.[23] The building, church home of the Saint Paul Methodists from 1924 to 1953, still stands at the Naples location although the original members moved to 4740 Lee Road in Cleveland, Ohio to form the Saint Paul United Methodist Church in 1954 (see Plate Number 5.1 for a photograph of the original church home of the Saint Paul Methodists).

Social Structure

The first acting pastor of the Saint Paul Methodist Church was the Reverend Edna Lee, beginning in 1923. The pastorate was shared with one Reverend Douglas whose first name was unknown. However, the Reverend Douglas in April of 1924 accepted a position with the Baptist Church.

While the membership grew slowly in the early years with rapid turnover in pastors, the development of the church since 1924 has been steady. Figure 5.1 helps to show the peaks and troughs in the growth of the congregation. From 1924 to 1929 the congregation grew from 30 to nearly 60 members, under the pastorates of the Reverend F.D. Lee (no relation to Reverend Edna Lee), April through September, 1924; and the Reverend John H. Simpson, September, 1924 through April, 1929. From 1929 to 1934, the membership declined from 60 to 48 individuals. The Reverend A.L. Holland, 1929-33, and the Reverend Andrew Johnson, 1933-34, were the pastors during this period.

In part, the growth shown during 1924-1929 may have marked the post-World War I period of expected new oppor-

THE VILLAGE

Plate 5.1

The Saint Paul Methodist Church
1924-1953, Naples Avenue
(The original wood-framed building still
stands, as shown below)

Source: Photograph taken by Wilbur H. Watson. August 21, 1984.

tunity in the world of work and improvement in the quality of family life of black immigrants from the southern United States coupled with the control of old Miles Heights by blacks and sympathetic whites. On the other hand, the period of declining membership from 1929-1934 may be accounted for, in part, by inducements for more out-migration than in-migration in THE VILLAGE brought about by the development of deepening financial indebtedness of old Miles Heights, difficulties in paying its public school teachers and keeping the school open, the crash of the stock market in 1929 and the first four years of the Great Depression. These factors may have influenced change in the congregations of the churches as well as the population of THE VILLAGE at large. (See Chapters Three and Seven for more detail on the plight of the school in THE VILLAGE.)

For reasons which are not stated in any available documents, membership of the Saint Paul Methodist Church stabilized from 1934-1937, holding constant at about 50 members. This period covered the one-year pastorate of the Reverend Horace White, April, 1934 through April, 1935, followed in 1935 by the return of Mrs. Edna Lee, who remained as pastor until she was forced to retire due to serious illness in June, 1940. As shown in Figure 5.1, the pastorate of the Reverend Lee, marked the sharpest period of growth in church membership since its beginning, from 50 to nearly 90 members. The period was marked also by gradual improvements in the economy, hope and opportunities brought by the Workmens' Progress Administration and the Social Security Act of 1935, as well as by the hard inspiritual work the Reverend Lee. According to Ferguson:

Figure 5.1

Growth in the Membership
of the Saint Paul Methodist Church,
1924-1950

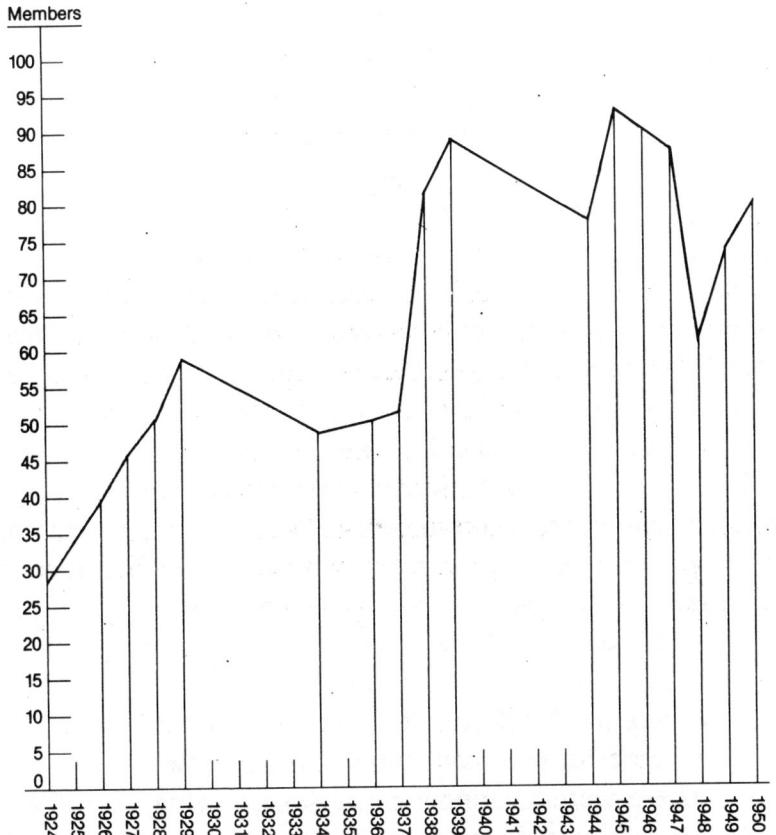

Source: Ferguson, John C. Unpublished history of Saint Paul Methodist Church. Cleveland, Ohio, **1953**, p. 13 (document made available by Mrs. Mildred Hall, Church Historian and Resident of THE VILLAGE).

> The records show that many were baptized and that a number of converts were added to the church. The outstanding achievements during this administration were the two additions made to the building and the construction of the basement. These improvements were made on the 'pay-as-you-go' plan. Most of the labor was donated by the men of the church and the community.[24]

Following the resignation of the Reverend Lee from active ministry in 1940, the Reverend O.B. Lindsey assumed the pastorate of the church. He remained in that position from June, 1940 through April 1948.[25]

Like the Reverend Lee, the Reverend Lindsey was credited with several baptisms. While there was a slight decline in membership from 1940-1944, offsetting growth occured between 1944 and 1947 before the onset of Lindsey's illness and subsequent retirement. As told by Ferguson, the Reverend Lindsey:

> ...Was the unfortunate victim of what may be termed as a 'transitional period.' There were a number of persons moving away from the community and a number engaging in defense work. So while the records may not show a large increase, they will show that a number of persons were added to the church during this administration.[26]

THE VILLAGE

In April of 1948, the Reverend John C. Ferguson, Jr. assumed the pastorate and served until 1953, when Saint Paul became a member of the United Methodist Church. As figure 5.1 shows, the membership increased from 1948 to 1950, the last year of documented change in membership in the historical statement composed by John C. Ferguson. Judging by the number of new members who joined the church under Ferguson, who had a kind of charismatic appeal similar to that which characterized the Reverends Edna S. Lee and O.B. Lindsey, it seemed reasonable to expect that the congregation would show steady growth during the years ahead.

The "Footwash" Baptist Church, 1923-1947

While several of the old-timers of THE VILLAGE have claimed the existence of a group called the "Footwash" Baptist Church in the early 1920's, research for this study has been unable to locate formal documents about this church. Nevertheless, the oral historical interviews suggest 1923 as the approximate date of establishment of the church.[27]

Through other oral historical interviews with former members whose kin and/or friends were members of the congregation, it has been possible to determine that the Reverend James Gary, Sr. was the first pastor of the "Footwash" Baptist Church. The place of worship was established in a small one room building in the early 1920's at the corner of Sunview and East 153rd, the current location of the New Home Baptist Church.[28] Interviews have also revealed that William Dark[29] and Wylie Sherman[30] served as deacons of the church during the ministry of the Reverend Gary. Information on the date of the demise of the church and/or its fusion with another congregation has not been discovered.

New Home Baptist Church 1947-Present

The founding members of the New Home Baptist Church were, until 1947, part of the congregation of the Canaan Missionary Baptist Church.[31] In that year conflict between two large factions within the Canaan congregation led to a split and the formation of "New Home."

The New Home group established its place of congregation and worship in a small wood frame building at the corner of Sunview Avenue and East 153rd Street in old Miles Heights. Although the building has undergone considerable renovation since 1947, the place of worship has remained at the original location. The current pastor (1986) is the Reverend Simpson Huggins, who had a membership of 145 persons as of 1982.[32]

Recent Developments Among Churches In THE VILLAGE

The Apostolic Church of The Living God occupies the former home of the Canaan Baptist Church at 14701 Ohio Avenue. It is under the pastorate of the Reverend Elder A. Burdette. Also included among churches that recently moved into THE VILLAGE are the original Church of God, located at the corner of Lincoln Avenue and East 153rd Street; the Church of the Assembly of Jesus Christ, at the corner of East 151st Street and Naples Avenue (formerly the location of the Saint Paul Methodists); the Pilgrim Community Church of

God, on Ohio Avenue since 1962, under the leadership of its founder and pastor, the Reverend Elizabeth Turner; and the Ebenezer Assembly (established in 1967) at 15209 Florida Avenue (formerly the Church of God), organized in 1935. The original building was destroyed by a tornado on October 10, 1966.[33]

Social Functions of the Church

Baptismal services were among the functions performed by each church for its members. While procreation is the primal means of population growth in human societies, baptism is the key to conversion, or "new birth" as a "child of God" in the Protestant religion.[34] In addition to baptism, conversion--or the ushering of the convert into a life of holiness, characterized by religious devotion, moral discipline, and missionary zeal--was induced through the following:

> Evangelical preaching [which] rejects the appeal to reason and restrained sensibilities for a direct, psychological assault upon sin and the equally direct and much more comforting offer of personal salvation. The style, suited as it is to the democracy of emotion rather than the hierarchy of intellect, destroys the psychological and social distance between preacher and people, often evoking tearful, passionate outbursts.[35]

Considering the harsh conditions of life in the rural southern and mid-western United States from which the early settlers came, the economic impoverishment of families, and the unimproved land upon which homes were developed in THE VILLAGE, it is no wonder that many families ritually turned to the message of hope provided by the ministries of the churches on their chosen days of worship.

Joining a church and achieving the sacrament of baptism were important to each new member of THE VILLAGE. For example, the absence of a baptismal pool in the building where the Canaan Baptists initially met in 1919 did not preclude the conduct of baptismal services. Instead a creek in a nearby wooded area located in old Miles Heights was used.[36] However, public protests developed about the unsanitary conditions of the creek and its use was banned by officials of Miles Heights village (around 1932). The leaders of the church then performed baptismal services at the Tried Stone Baptist Church at 40th and Scollville Avenue, five miles away, in Cleveland.[37]

In 1953 Canaan succeeded in having its own pool built in. However, in 1978 when the church moved to its current home at East 162nd Street in the City of Cleveland, it was once again without baptismal facilities. Until August, 1986 when Canaan once again constructed a new pool, the pastor used for baptismal purposes Lee-Seville Baptist Church, at 4831 Lee Road in Cleveland.[38]

Reinforcing intra-familial bonds was another important function of the church. Providing a place for family and kin to gather, "count their blessings," and renew vows to work and live together in harmony has been one of the most important social functions of the church in society.[39] Dubois observed in his study of "Negro Churches" in a predominantly black county in the state of Georgia, 1903, that a large proportion of the congregations could be characterized as "family churches."[40]

A study of the lists of surnames and matching addresses for members of the Saint Paul Methodist Church, 1950-52 tended to corroborate DuBois' characterization of rural black congregations as "family churches." The membership roll showed that among 69 members, including two who were on the "preparatory roll" and one on the "constituency roll," fully 64 percent, or 44 individuals, shared membership in the church as part of a family group. On this list the size of family groups ranged from a minimum of two (2) to a maximum of seven (7).[41] This finding suggests the persistence of the significance of the church as a pillar of the community among blacks during the previous half century.

According to Frazier,[42] for many decades the church represented the only organized social existence for blacks outside of the family. Frazier observed that:

> Rural Negro communities in the South were named after their churches. In fact, the Negro population in the rural South has been organized in 'church communities' which represented their widest social orientation and the largest social groups in which they found an identification. Moreover, since the Negro was an outsider in the American

community, it was the church that enlisted his deepest loyalties. Therefore, it was more than an amusing incident to note some years ago in a rural community in Alabama, that a Negro when asked to identify the people in the adjoining community replied: 'The nationality there is Methodist.' ...For the Negro masses, in their social and moral isolation in American society, the Negro church community has been a nation within a nation.[43]

The Church as a Source of News and a Means of Reaffirming Neighborhood Solidarity

Whether or not there were intense beliefs in the creeds of the religion of the community church, many blacks attended nevertheless. In many small black churches, including those in the VILLAGE, a portion of time was allocated on each day of worship for the minister or church secretary to chronicle the news of events that happened since the last church meeting, especially but not exclusively, pertaining to members. Racial separatism in the United States and between VILLAGE insiders and whites in the surrounding environment had much to do with the development of the church as a community center for gathering among neighbors.

> Whether or not they derive any particular joy there from, the Negroes must go to church, to see their friends, as they are barred from social centers open to

whites. They must attend, moreover, to find out what is going on; for the race has not sufficient interests to maintain in every locality a newspaper of its own, and the white dailies generally mention Negroes only when they happen to commit crimes against white persons. The young Negro must go to church to meet his sweet heart, to impress her with his worth and woo her in marriage; the Negro farmer to find out the developments in the business world; the Negro mechanic to learn the needs of his community and how he may supply them.[44]

Based upon Fausett's study of *Black Gods of the Metropolis*, there is yet another function of the black church, especially for church leaders and other ambitious members of Afro-American religious groups. The church functions as a *place for meetings conducive to developing business and political interest groups among blacks.*[45]

Under the conditions of racial segregation in the United States during the first half of the twentieth century, the pressures for goods and services set in motion a series of demands by blacks that hardly could be met by any outlet other than black owned and operated businesses. The demands of black consumers became the backbone for many small businesses owned and operated by blacks, such as those described in Chapter 6 of this book.[46]

In addition to helping to account for the development of small businesses among blacks, racial segregation and aspirations of blacks to survive in spite of it may also help to account for the persistence and economic success of some businesses, in spite of downturns in the economy such as the Great Depression of the 1930s. According to Fausett, while it was not unusual for blacks in the southern United States during the first half of the twentieth century to have "amassed considerable wealth in business, particularly in real estate, insurance, in the trades, and in the professions," largely due to de facto and de jure segregation and a relative absence of "cultural life" outside the ghetto, the competition of whites in the North narrowly restricted blacks "even within the limits of [their] own racial group."[47] As a result of the more intense competition and the more pervasive influence of whites on blacks in the North, even within the segregated "black communities," the church became one of the few--and at times, the only--institutional bulwark and organized group through which blacks could find a solid means of supporting each other politically and economically. "By making it possible for agencies to be established to fulfill those needs, it [the church] tends to transform these urges into the imperatives of American culture."[48] For example, in THE VILLAGE the Reverend Moore of the Canaan Missionary Baptist Church developed and operated a small neighborhood store on the edge of the property owned by the church:

> "...Reverend Moore ran a store. Right down at the end of Lincoln, where it dead ends. He ran a little confectionery candy store. Most customers were church

members. He and his wife lived on Ohio."[49]

Reverend Moore's corner store was a microcosm of efforts by church leaders with more resources in other black communities during the early twentieth century. While some ministers were building large, beautiful edifices as monuments to their deities and successful leadership, others were trying to improve their efficiency in church management and to find ways to help the poor in their communities. There developed through churches in Pittsburgh, Chicago, and Cleveland, such as the Antioch Baptist Church, credit unions, "organized banks, housing corporations, insurance companies, and even steamship projects."[50] These facts reinforce the importance assigned the church by Frazier, who claimed that for decades extending into the twentieth century in many communities, "the church was the only organized social existence" outside the family.[51]

Partly as a consequence of racial segregation, although probably unwittingly so far as white segregationists were concerned, the black church became a source of support for blacks by providing a springboard for those aspiring to political as well as economic goals which otherwise might have been denied them in the secular world. As Woodson noted in his observations of the perspectives of whites on blacks in the early twentieth century, "There are in the south today white men who regret that immediately after the Civil War, they permitted the Negro to establish their separate churches."[52] As churches increasingly revealed truths about white exploitation of blacks and lead movements against racial oppression, the heirs of the former "master class" became increasingly critical of black members of the clergy. Yet, until the Civil Rights Movements of the 1960's, they were constrained by custom and law in some places from interferring with speech making, especially in the church, and movements led by black preachers.[53] In 1964 in Mississippi alone, whites bombed or burned 34 black churches.[54]

Until the 1960's, black preachers in the South were permitted greater freedom of speech and allowed to exercise more influence than any other black leaders in their communities.[55] There was evidence of constraint, however, of speech reflected through sermons especially in the South that avoided violating the segregationist interests of the early Twentieth century. Pinkney makes the following distinctions between black preachers, south and north:

> The frustrations inherent in the lives of Black Americans were such that some form of outlet was essential. The character of black religion being what it was, that is, concerned with other-worldly matters, meant that it posed no serious threat to established patterns of white supremacy. Therefore religious activity among Negroes was not only tolerated but encouraged. The minister could be trusted, and the church served to contain the black masses. In the north, where white supremacy was less well institutionalized, the black church remained somewhat more independent. Unlike their

southern counterparts, nothern black ministers were more responsive to the needs of their followers than to the white community. Therefore, they were more likely to become involved in the politics of the larger community, and they frequently became leaders in opposition to segregation and discrimination against blacks.[56]

While THE VILLAGE was located in Ohio, a northern state as it were, there was no evidence of church leaders taking public stands against segregation and discrimination as described by Pinkney. The sermons read during this study were closer in substance and emphasis to Woodson's and Pinkney's characterizations of the southern black preacher and church. The church, nevertheless, served important leadership and integrative functions within the black community.

Spiritual rebirth and the nurturing of a sense of unity among community members were clearly two of the most significant social functions of the church. The provision of places to release tensions through singing and shouting, to organize and convene political meetings without the risk of intrusion by outsiders and to learn about and offer aid to minimize suffering of some families were also important contributions of the church.

Teaching elementary skills in reading and writing through Bible school and other small group activities were also of considerable importance. In reference to the church in Black communities throughout the United States, Carter G. Woodson sets this observation in broader perspective:

> ....They studied in the churches on Sunday, learned the alphabet, the spelling of words with one, two, and three syllables, and finally to read the Bible, that they might know for themselves the truths hitherto kept from their fathers but now revealed to their children in freedom.... Many of these Negroes often learned more on a single Sunday than the average student acquired in a day school during the week....The majority of Negroes became Bible readers. Reading the Bible, they not only found out what a minister of limited education could point out, but facts drawn from the best thought of the ancient world.... Some [went on to] read books on ancient and medieval history, and finally works on the history of modern Europe.[57]

The teaching function is especially significant when consideration is given the fact that there was only one public school in the entire Miles Heights area and that the students periodically had only half day schedules. It should also be noted that the mere presence of Sunday Schools and other teaching services did not themselves distinguish black from non-black churches. Instead, the distinction was (1) the dual function of these services as in developing basic skills in the uses of the English language as well as in teaching biblical lessons for an illiterate oppressed people who happened to be black, and (2) the larger number of black churches which reported conducting Sunday Schools. For example, whereas 79 percent of all church organizations regardless of race reported Sunday Schools in 1906, 91 percent of all black churches reported them.[58] As previous studies have documented for other black communities,[59] the church in the history and social organization of THE VILLAGE has been a major force helping to sustain family life and buttress community organization overall.

Conclusions

This chapter shows the development of the church as an integral institution of THE VILLAGE. It also shows how each church functioned to provide refuge from despair, account for the uncertainties of life in a harsh economic and socially oppressive environment (especially outside THE VILLAGE), and inspire hope and renewed confidence to face the challenges of everyday life. While the Canaan Missionary Baptist Church (1919) is the oldest in THE VILLAGE, followed by the founding of the St. Paul Methodist Church in 1921, each of these groups and several others that emerged thereafter contributed to the overall stability and growth of THE VILLAGE.

There was a close link between the church and family life of VILLAGERS. While members of some family groups tended to select church memberships that were not shared by other family members, the membership records of the two oldest churches showed that the congregations tended to be constituted by family groups. Within any given church membership, there were two or more members from a family, but not necessarily married couples of the same family group.

Clearly, the church was an important institution in THE VILLAGE, with social functions extending far beyond the contributions of the church to the religious life of the people. It was the emergence of the family and church centered lives of VILLAGERS within a racially segregated and oppressive society that also framed the social and cultural context for the development of small businesses in THE VILLAGE.

Chapter 6

PRIVATE ENTERPRISE

To take away any considerable part of the customary livelihood of a mass of people means that their ingenuity will be stimulated to find new avenues of labor if they are really energetic and resourceful. The Philadelphia (and THE VILLAGE) Negroes were energetic. They had established their own churches and beneficial societies, they had accumulated some property, they had sent their children to school, and they were not willing to be simply and always servants and common laborers (DuBois, 1901).[1]

While the early years of THE VILLAGE were characterized by rapid in-migration of new settlers attracted by the war works industries of Cleveland, its economic growth was brought to a grinding halt by the Depression of the 1930's. One of the most poignant illustrations of the economic strains brought by the Depression was found in the plight of the administration of old Miles Heights under the newly installed black mayor. Arthur R. Johnston's first year as mayor (1929) coincided with the collapse of the stock market and the near collapse of Beehive School, the only institution for public education in old Miles Heights. In spite of the economic hardships, however, THE VILLAGERS found many enterprising ways to sustain themselves.

From the oral historical accounts of some of the earliest settlers of THE VILLAGE still living at the time of this study, the Protestant ethic in the early nineteen twenties still strongly motivated business development. In his classical sociological treatise on *The Protestant Ethic and the Spirit of Capitalism*, Max Weber (1958) summarized the essential ethical features which, when incorporated into everyday thought and action, tend to be associated closely with economic success. These features include:

> The religious valuation of restless, continuous, systematic work in a worldly calling, as the highest means to asceticism, and at the same time the surest and most evident proof of rebirth and genuine faith,...have been the most powerful conceivable levers for the expansion of that attitude toward life which we have here called the spirit of capitalism.[2]

As early as 1925 an estimated one hundred Afro-American and approximately ten Italian and German families lived in the subsection of Miles Heights called THE VILLAGE. According to old-timers, also at least two general stores there sold groceries, household, and garden supplies. These were (1) the Scott Store, on Sunview Avenue, and (2) the A.C. Williams store, located in a two story building at the corner of Naples and East 151st Street. The A.C. Williams store was distinguished by an outlet for groceries, an icecream parlor and other goods on the first floor, and a dance hall and room for community meetings on the second floor.

THE VILLAGE

In spite of or because of the Great Depression, new businesses developed along with in-migration of new families in THE VILLAGE in the 1930's. "Boot-leg joints" (illegal manfacturers and distributors of alcoholic beverages) already were present by the 1920's, as previously noted by Mrs. Anna Johnston, the late wife of former mayor Johnston.[3]

It was probably no coincidence that the crash of the stock market in 1929 and the subsequent deepening of economic depression through the 1930's were accompanied by the opening of new boot-leg joints as well as two new taverns in THE VILLAGE. Similar patterns in the relationship between economic decline and a rise in liquor sales may be seen in other small depressed towns in the United States. "Link's Tavern" on Sunview Avenue (now known as "Bea's"), and "Hobart's Saloon" at the corner of Naples Avenue and 151st Street (which went out of business in 1944) opened in the late 1930's and early 40's.

The late 1930's also marked the opening of "Tallie's Store," an Italian owned and operated general store on Ohio Avenue across the street from the entrance to East 144th Street. In that same decade (1930's), the Wells-Oatman store, black owned and operated, opened its doors in 1931 on Sunview Avenue at the corner of East 151st Street. Subsequently (1933), Oatman's Grocery Store moved to its present location at the corner of Lawndale and East 153st Street.[4]

Small Businesses

The presence of boot-leg joints in old Miles Heights was a source of consternation to former Mayor Johnston. Moreover

BUSINESS

Plate 6.1.

The building that housed the A. C. Williams Store dates from 1917, the oldest black owned business in THE VILLAGE. This building still stands, although unoccupied, at the corner of East 151st and Florida Avenue.

Source: Photograph taken by Wilbur H. Watson, August 22, 1984

the public outrage against operators of these distributors of liquid "spirits" inspired Johnston to commit his administration to put them out of business. In spite of public outrage, however, the period during and since Johnston's term as mayor has shown a continuing presence of these businesses in THE VILLAGE. It may well be that these places of ill-repute, of which four have been identified by current residents of THE VILLAGE, are among the more enduring institutions performing social and psychological functions not met by other institutions in small low income settlements like THE VILLAGE.

With the rapid growth of the population and the coming of the Great Depression, several new businesses emerged. Included among them was the first Tavern (1933), popularly known as Ruby's and Link's place, that was licensed to sell beer and wine over-the-counter for consumption on the premises. Between 1930 and 1942 a total of five small businesses emerged in THE VILLAGE with licenses to sell alcholic beverages. In addition to Ruby's & Link's Place, there was Wilson's Place, 1939; "Link's Beer Parlor", 1939; "Hobart's Tavern," 1941; and "Elie's," 1942.[5] By 1984, however, only "Link's Beer Parlor" (now known as "Bea's") was still licensed to sell beer and wine over-the-counter for consumption on or off the premises. The reasons for the demise of the other dispensers of liquid spirits varied. Hobart's and Napier's are now closed entirely. Elie's still operates a grocery store and sells beer and wine as packaged goods, but is no longer licensed to sell liquor over-the counter.[6]

The decline of liquor licenses was accompanied by an increase in the number of churches in THE VILLAGE from one, the Canaan Missionary Baptist Church in 1919, to six (6) in 1984. While this study has not demonstrated a relationship between the rise of clergymen and their congregations and the decline of liquor licenses, it does not follow that there is no relationship. The emphasis is on licensed establishments because there is still a thriving business of boot-leg joints in THE VILLAGE. This means that the major decline has been in businesses licensed to sell liquor to the public, not in the private and underground sale of it.

Peddlers

In addition to the grocery stores, taverns and the other businesses discussed above, there was a variety of peddlers in THE VILLAGE. A peddler is a street vendor who travels about, usually within an area bounded by certain streets, with various goods and services for sale.

Among the goods sold by peddlers in THE VILLAGE were blocks of ice, heating coal, fresh fruit and groceries, including fresh meat, fish, and some diary products. Because peddlers in the 1920's, 30's and 40's tended to be poor and without modern refrigerated trucks, many were restricted in the quantity of perishable foods that could be carried for sale on any given day.

In addition to the distinctions among peddlers based upon the goods and services offered, they can be distinguished by the techniques used to draw attention and induce customer interest in their goods. Among peddlers in THE VILLAGE, two broad categories were distinguished by their promotional techniques: These were *passive vendors* and *hawkers*. While perhaps not deliberately intended, all street vendors in THE VILLAGE were male.

In the conduct of business, the *passive vendor* tended to restrict himself (or be restricted) to an established route or street corner location and customers who regularly patronized his business. In personality and practice, the *passive vendor* was relatively unaggressive, or not outgoing. Because of these characteristics he was not very competitive and tended not to do well in an open market with other vendors who were more aggressive. However, if a *passive vendor*, such as the late "Doc Williford," happened to specialize (as he did) in the sale of fresh garden vegetables and fruit that were in high demand and not offered by his competition, then he could be expected to do well economically in spite of his passive approach to promotion.

Along with his wife and children, Doc moved to old Miles Heights in 1928, initially settling on Lincoln Avenue. During the growing season (June - September) Doc's day was organized around farming eight (8) acres of land and raising pigs for the market. As a peddler, he worked from a horse-drawn buckboard on which the vegetables and fruit for sale were attractively arranged. In his daily peddling, there were certain regular customers whom he would see and others who might hail him along the way, stopping to make selected purchases.

Plate 6.2

Likeness of Vendors Using Horsedrawn Carriages, 1920-1950

Source: J. D. Smith, former resident of THE VILLAGE and Associate Pastor of the Canaan Missionary Baptist Church, June 25, 1984.

Other *passive vendors* included "Spot" Gray, who peddled home heating coal in THE VILLAGE. While Gray lived in THE VILLAGE on Naples Avenue, he worked for and peddled coal supplied by a company outside THE VILLAGE. According to an old timer, "Spot's" Christian name was Max.[6] He became known as "Spot" among VILLAGE folks because of his very dark complexion. It should also be noted, according to another VILLAGER who once worked for Gray, that he was one of the first peddlers to modernize his delivery service by trading in his horse and buckboard for a small pick-up truck (date unknown).[7]

Johnnie Harris, also a peddler, was a *hawker*, in contrast to Williford and Gray. He was distinguished from Doc also by his sale of blocks of ice and heating coal, and only secondarily did he sell fresh vegetables and fruit. As such, whether by design or accident, these vendors complemented each other much more than they competed.

According to the old timers who assisted me as informants, Harris also peddled from a horsedrawn wagon at least as early as 1925. Unlike Doc Williford, Harris would call out at the top of his voice to let residents know that he was approaching their homes. Calling out, clanging a bell, blowing a whistle or using other techniques deliberately designed to draw the attention of consumers is the distinguishing characteristic of hawking. It is true that the *hawker* may have established customers and may not have needed to be theatrical to induce sales, but those prospects did not diminish the practice of hawking nor the attention-getting advantage that acrued to the vendor who used it.

"The Fishman," who also lived in THE VILLAGE and whose family name was Jewell Anthony, was also a *hawker* who specialized in the sale of fish and other seafoods in THE VILLAGE.[8] He would catch fresh fish daily through his own skills and tools, usually rod, reel and net, then bring his catch to THE VILLAGE for sale. Unlike other vendors in THE VILLAGE, he would peddle from the trunk of his car, or simply walk the street with his catch in a sack.[9]

Finally, acknowledgment must be given the combined peddling and delivery services of the Oatman Store. While this store was one of the oldest outlets for processed foods in THE VILLAGE, it also sold blocks of ice, heating coal, kerosene, gasoline, bottled beer and wine and a variety of other goods and services.[10] Moreover, the owners of the Oatman Store were known for their aggressive pursuit of opportunities for expansion. It was not surprising, therefore, to find the store operating a home delivery service system. This service combined the delivery of bags of groceries, loads of ice, coal and other goods on request to specific homes as well as hawking other goods that could be loaded on the wagon for the journey through the streets.

Modern Technology, the Rise of Corporate Utilities and the Decline of Small Business in THE VILLAGE

The rise of public utility companies, especially electric and gas, have emerged since 1900 and gradually spread from urban to rural areas, displacing peddlers of ice, heating coal, kerosene and other substances previously used to produce creature comforts in nonindustrial societies such as THE

THE VILLAGE

VILLAGE. Like other small communities largely peopled by poor families, many of the residents of THE VILLAGE could not afford to avail themselves of the services of the expanding utility companies. Some continued to use wood and coal burning stoves, kerosene lamps, and iceboxes well into the 1950's and 60's. The constraints on resident consumption of utility services clearly resulted from a lack of economic means, not the absence of need nor appreciation of the conveniences that would result from the use of the services.

Other Small Businesses

The manufacture of cinder blocks for use in the construction of houses, retainer walls, and other projects was one of the more innovative businesses of the Oatman family. According to a member of the family, this business developed and functioned over approximately an eight (8) year period from 1939-1947.[11] As told by an old-timer who lived in THE VILLAGE and was kin to the Oatman family, the senior Matthew Oatman actually devised the technique of manufacturing cinder blocks through his own ingenuity. This old-timer described the procedure as follows:

> "Sand, cement and granulated slag screening were poured into a mixing machine, then water was added. This mixture was poured into steel molds, eight inches wide and eight inches deep. After the cement was poured in the molds, a gasoline operated machine with pods designed to fit each mold was ac-

activated to press the cement firmly into each mold."[12]

Other small businesses included "Zunk's" Restaurant, 1957-65, at the corner of Florida and East 153rd Street. The building that housed this restaurant was demolished in 1960. Minnifies Moving Service (East 147th Street), Dickerson's Beauty Parlor (Sunview Avenue, next to Bea's Place), and "Little John's" (Cornelius) Body Shop at 15221 Sunview Avenue (1943-49), were also among the small businesses that once operated in THE VILLAGE.[13]

There is no doubt that the decline of selected small businesses, such as coal peddling, was due partly to the rise in income, modern technology, and the expansion of the services of utility companies from urban centers into the urban fringe. The rise of supermarkets and malls of retail stores for the sale of groceries, clothing, drugs, hardware, household, and other goods, the development of mass public transportation systems, and the increasing acquisition of automobiles by families also contributed to the decline of resident dependency on local small businesses. In 1944, pre-fabricated homes for war veterans and their families were installed on the east side of East 153rd and the south side of Seville Road in THE VILLAGE. Then in 1946, additional war housing was added to the "Seville Homes" development on the north side of Seville Road along with a small shopping mall. To accomodate the need of the growing population in the area for mass transit, especially a vehicular bridge between THE VILLAGE and the City of Cleveland, the Cleveland Transit System installed a shuttle bus service in 1947.[14] These and other

THE VILLAGE

developments which are described in more detail in Chapter 7 have had a substantial impact on THE VILLAGE.

The Seville Homes mall closed with the decline of the local public housing project that was torn down in 1958,[15] and most of the small businesses described above did not resurface. Only Bea's Tavern, the Oatman Grocery Store (which closed in 1988), and Elie's General Store withstood the social and technological changes of recent decades and still operate in THE VILLAGE. As told to me by the late Mrs. Martha Oatman, the success of her store and perhaps Elie's, which sells similar goods, probably is related to the owners' sensitivity to changing times and demands for new products which they are able to accommodate.[16]

The persistence of Bea's Tavern and various boot-leg joints clearly is related to the ageless need of some men and women to achieve periodically, by one means or another, psychological release from the demands of everyday life. According to a member of the family that operates Bea's Tavern and a number of local residents, these are the only public places in THE VILLAGE where people can go for recreation.[17] For some, the presence and/or consumption of alcoholic beverages on the premises of these places is secondary to other social functions provided by them. For example, for young adults in particular, the consumption of alcoholic beverages is not the primary reason for their patronage of Bea's and similar places; it is the opportunity to meet new and old friends, make new acquaintances, and play pinball machines and table games such as pool, poker, and chess that are provided by the owner.

Conclusion

The development and perserverance of private enterprise in THE VILLAGE help to show another side of the internal order of the black community. The proprietors of these businesses and their customers, especially those who lived there, were intricately bound to each other. Mutual support and neighborhood ties contributed to the economic, social and psychological sustenance of each.

In Chapters 2 through 6, beginning with a focus on early settlers and family life in THE VILLAGE, the interdependence of the basic institutions and the changing social, political, and economic contexts of this small community from the early twentieth century to the present has been shown. In addition to documenting the history and organization of the community itself, as originally intended, Chapter 3 raised into bold relief the mayoralty and other political achievements of Arthur R. Johnston. The next chapter summarizes the study overall and draws general conclusions.

Table 6.1

CHRONOLOGY OF SMALL BUSINESSES IN THE VILLAGE BY DATE, NAME, LOCATION AND OWNERSHIP

Date	Name of Business	Location	Ownership
1917	A. C. Williams Store	Corner of Florida Avenue and East 151st Street	A.C. Williams[18]
1933-38	Ruby's/Link's Place	"	Ruby Brooks and Link Gresham[19]
1939-41	Wilson's Place	"	West Wilson
1941-44	Hobart's Place	"	Hobart Murray
--	Napier	"	Napier Family
--	Kelley's	"	Owner's name unknown

Table 6.1 (Continued)

Date	Name of Business	Location	Ownership
1920's	Scott's Store[20] ("Black and White Scott Store", a folkname attributed to the store because Scott married a white woman.)	Sunview Avenue	John Scott
1925's	Will Anderson (grocery store)	Naples Avenue (near dead end)	Will Anderson[21,22]
1928-54	Williford's Groceries (included peddling from a horsedrawn carriage)	Lincoln Avenue	Doc Williford[23]

Table 6.1 (Continued)

Date	Name of Business	Location	Ownership
1931-33	Wells-Oatman Store (bought store from Rose Jenkins Scott whose husband previously had a store at the same location)[24]	15010 Sunview Avenue	Daley Wells and Matthew Oatman
1933-88	Oatman's Grocery Store	15229 Lawndale Avenue	Matthew Oatman
1939-47	Oatman's Building Supplies: Manufacturing of Cinder Blocks	15229 Lawndale Avenue	Matthew Oatman
1937-39	"Link's" Place (pool room & gasoline pump)	15134 Sunview Avenue	Gresham family[26]
1939-present	"Link's" Beer Parlor	15134 Sunview Avenue	Gresham family[27]

Table 6.1 (Continued)

Date	Name of Business	Location	Ownership
1938-48	"Tallies" Store	Ohio Avenue	Owner's name unknown
1941-52	"Link's" Grocery Store	15134 Sunview Avenue	Gresham family[26]
1939-59	Henderson's Cleaners	Naples Avenue	Henderson Family
1942-present	Elie's Store	Ohio Avenue	Oliver Elie[25]
1944-55	Hobart's Tavern	Corner of Naples & East 151 Street	Hobart Murray[29]
1955-56	Ringside Cafe	"	Nate Brooks
1947-53	"Shoemaker George"	East 151st Street (behind Elie's)	John Williams
1947-53	Sander's TV Shop	East 151st Street	Owner's name unknown

Chapter 7

SUMMARY AND CONCLUSIONS

Old Miles Heights no longer exists as it did during its heyday from 1917 to 1980. This period saw the founding of Beehive School (1917), the rise to political power of Arthur R. Johnston, probably best known for his term as Mayor of old Miles Heights Village between 1929 and 1931, the death of Johnston in 1957, and the closing of Beehive School in 1980.

THE VILLAGE, the predominantly black subsection of old Miles Heights, also has undergone significant social change. The street boundaries, however, of THE VILLAGE proper, as shown in Plate Number 2.2 (Chapter 2), remain the same. The extension of full water and sewer services to the VILLAGE area in 1954, the expansion of the Cleveland Transit System in 1955 to include THE VILLAGE, and the dismantling in 1958 of the Lee-Seville Homes for veterans of World War II converged to mark an end to nearly a half century of isolation of the people of this settlement on the southeastern border of Cleveland.

THE VILLAGE itself also has undergone extensive modernization. The development of new housing for middle-income families that began in 1980 and plans of the City of Cleveland for a new industrial park including private homes to be located in the area where the Lee-Seville public housing project once stood portend further modernization of housing, shopping districts, street and lighting improvements, and new small businesses. Nevertheless, THE VILLAGE remains today an all black community.

CONCLUSIONS

The Beehive School, 1917-1980

One of the earliest signs of community organization in the old Miles Heights area was the founding of the Beehive School in 1917. The term *area* of old Miles Heights is used because as an incorporated village Miles Heights was not founded until 1925, while Beehive School was established by the Commissioners of Warrensville Township twelve years earlier. Warrensville Township subsumed the land area that subsequently became Miles Heights village.

Perhaps because of the closeness of the founding of Beehive School and Miles Heights village, many old-timers and not-so-old-timers have confused old Miles Heights and Beehive, as if the two institutions had identical dates of origin. With the incorporation of Miles Heights village in 1925, the Beehive School district that previously had the same boundaries as Miles Heights became the school system that provided for the educational needs of this growing suburban village.

Beehive School rose from a small schoolhouse during World War I to a three story school building in 1925 on Lee Road near the intersection of Lee and Miles Avenue. By 1925 the school was large enough to accommodate 700 children, grades K through 12, with 22 teachers. The student body numbered approximately 700 from 1925 to 1932, when the Beehive School District was annexed to the Cleveland School District. The change in school district affiliation, however, did not mean the demise of Beehive School.

THE VILLAGE

Under the Cleveland School District, Beehive was reorganized. Beginning in 1932 its classroom offerings were restricted to grades K through 8, with Alexander Hamilton and Moses Cleveland Junior High Schools becoming the educational institutions to which most students went upon graduation from Beehive School.

During the period from 1932 to 1980, a variety of other changes occurred. Physical plant renovation, curriculum revision, and changes in philosophy with each new principal were among them. For two years following its closing in 1980, the old Beehive School building remained vacant. But in 1983 it was purchased by a group of local businessmen who converted the facility into a complex of apartments for senior citizens. Today (1988), it remains a housing unit for seniors known as the Beehive School Apartments.

The Mayoralty of Arthur R. Johnston
(1929-1931)

The most distinguished social and political event in the history of THE VILLAGE and old Miles Heights was the rise of Arthur R. Johnston, who won election to the office of mayor of Miles Heights village in 1929. As shown in Chapter 3, the predominantly black VILLAGE from which Johnston sprang was included in the political district that was incorporated in 1925 as Miles Heights village, a subdivision of Warrensville Township, Ohio.

Johnston, a black man who immigrated to the United States from Jamaica in the early 20th century, married in 1916 after serving two years in the United States army and settled in the VILLAGE in 1919. A pleasant personality, charismatic leadership that appealed to blacks and whites, and support of the Republican party, won Johnston election to the founding Council of Miles Heights in 1927. He subsequently was elected to the presidency of the Miles Heights Council (1928), and to the mayor's office in 1929.

While Johnston's mayoralty was tainted by charges of political corruption among other elected and appointed officials in his administration, financially troubled schools, and delinquent tax receipts of residents of Miles Heights village, these problems and others do not diminish the importance of his achievements, especially considering the nature of race relations and the political and economic oppression of blacks that were so widespread in the United States following World War I. Race relations and civil rights laws, however, have changed significantly in the United States since the 1920's. The annexation of Miles Heights village to the City of Cleveland in early 1932, and the annexation of the Beehive School District to the Cleveland School District late in the same year helped to mark the end of Miles Heights village as an incorporated political district with taxing powers and a mayor-council form of government.

Economic Conditions

With the coming of the Depression of the 1930s, there was widespread economic hardship for the people of THE VILLAGE. Poverty, however, was not new to the black inhabitants. Most had come just a few years earlier from economically depressed rural areas of the southern United States, and in some instances VILLAGERS had migrated from poor inner city ghettoes of Cleveland, Chicago, Detroit, Indianapolis, and Louisville after previous residence in one or more of those cities. The great majority, however, traced their roots to one or more of the states in the "black belt" of the United States.

As shown in Chapters 2 through 6, VILLAGERS found a variety of ways of coping with the difficulties of everyday life, of which poverty was a major challenge. Pooling their meagre resources during the 1920s and 1930s to form networks of mutual social and economic support was foremost among their coping techniques.

With the coming of World War II and growth in the economy of greater Cleveland, some VILLAGERS also began to realize improvements in their economic state. From the middle to the end of World War II and the gradual return of war veterans to the Cleveland area, pressures developed for new housing to shelter the veterans and their families. In 1944 the Cleveland metropolitan war-housing development completed a project in the Seville area, just East of 153rd Street (the Eastern border of THE VILLAGE), and South of Seville Road. These temporary homes provided dwelling units for 2,039 individuals at a cost of $1,623,166.[2] As war veterans continued to return to the Cleveland area, the demand for new housing increased.

In 1946, the Cleveland Metropolitan Housing Authority opened several new temporary housing projects for "in-migrant war workers," including the "Seville Homes Extension" project.[3] To facilitate the social adjustment and meet the educational needs of the new families of the Seville

Homes, a new elementary school, Clara Tag Brewer, was constructed in the area in 1947. In addition to public housing and the new elementary school, the Seville Homes development included physical plants for supportive services, such as a shopping mall that included a grocery store, a drug store, and a separate building for a recreation center. The Seville Homes housing units remained until 1958, when the families were ordered to vacate the premises for demolition.

Extending Mass Transit Services to THE VILLAGE

In addition to the new elementary school, the Cleveland Transit System (that was subsumed in 1984 under the Regional Transit Authority of the Cleveland Metropolitan Area) initiated in 1947 a shuttle bus service between the end of the transit line at East 131st Street and Miles Avenue, and the junction of Seville Road and East 153rd Street. Like many other small rural towns, especially in the southern United States, until very recently THE VILLAGE was cut off by the absence of regular mass transportation services from the nearest urban center, Cleveland and from its markets, financial institutions, and other services. The Regional Transit Authority did not extend regular bus services to THE VILLAGE until 1954.[4] Before this service, the residents of THE VILLAGE were left to their own devices, including walking, "jitney" services, and thumbing rides when needed. Since 1954, the Regional Transit Authority has extended mass transit services to Seville and Lee Road (March, 1955), then to East 177th and Miles (March, 1963) where the bus service currently ends in the Lee-Seville area.[5]

THE VILLAGE

Yesterday, Today, and Tomorrow

Few of the original settlers still live in THE VILLAGE. Their paths of outmigration have led some to purchase or rent housing in inner city Cleveland, or suburban and urban fringe settlements where land was available for farming as well as developing new households. Other VILLAGERS, and the offspring of first generation African Americans who originally established residence there have left the VILLAGE since World War II to return to the southeastern United States. Perhaps one of the most significant migratory symbols of change was the exit early in 1988 of Arthur R. Johnston's oldest surviving daughter, who moved from THE VILLAGE to a senior citizens complex in Cleveland.

Even though outmigration has been considerable since World War II, many former VILLAGERS still hold fond memories of days gone by. Reverie, renewing old ties through club meetings and annual reunions, and gathering news about the successes and failures of former residents through frequent telephone talk and occasional encounters in markets and other public places help THE VILLAGERS keep in touch with one another. Regular meetings of social clubs, such as the NUCLEUS, the annual reunions of VILLAGERS, and other activities deliberately organized by new and old-timers help considerably to sustain common positive sentiments and reinforce the sense of belonging.

Family migration and settlement tends to be accompanied by the diffusion of beliefs, values, and systems of religious faith acquired by members over time. And like the soul of a society that is sustained through the relations among its people, especially among true believers, selected churches also are sustained over time. Included among churches of THE VILLAGE which have survived are the Canaan Missionary Baptist Church and the St. Paul Methodist Church, the two oldest churches of THE VILLAGE. Although the physical plant of each is now located on the periphery of THE VILLAGE boundaries shown in Plate Number 2.2 (Chapter 2), many of the members of the congregations are still drawn from among current and former residents of THE VILLAGE.

All indications are that THE VILLAGE of yesterday will continue to undergo modernization in the future. Ground breaking for new single family housing was begun in 1980 in the area of the old Lee Seville Homes, and the construction of other new housing was begun in the same general area in 1984. New streets and sewers already have been cut and paved in the area where a small industrial park and mall are planned along with new housing priced for the middle classes. Residents in the old section shown on Plate #2.2 increasingly are renovating and improving their homes. Since the inception of this study, although not necessarily because of it, the City of Cleveland has chosen to recognize the distinctive achievements of Arthur R. Johnston by naming a small recreation park in his name at the dead-end of East 147th Street near the home where he lived from 1919 until his death. More recently, in 1984, the City completed a new street through the old Seville Homes land area also named in honor of Johnston: "Arthur R. Johnston Boulevard." Sixty years later, Arthur R. Johnston has begun to receive the attention that he richly deserves. Although in a minor key, this study and the recent public events in honor of Arthur R. Johnston help to show the significance of work in revisionist history and careful sociological inquiry in combination with public education interest groups as forces helping to induce social change.

The next Chapter, on "The Social Construction of Social History," discusses a variety of questions and some propositions about social, political, and individual factors that help frame the context of social science inquiry and decision making processes in the reconstruction of history. The aim is to examine further factors that help account for the omission previously of Johnston and old Miles Heights in histories of blacks in Cleveland, Cuyahoga County, and Ohio, and some of the methodological problems involved in revisionist historical research in general.

CHAPTER 8

AFTERWORD: ON THE SOCIAL CONSTRUCTION OF SOCIAL HISTORY

The science of history has the momentous task of deciding which events, actions, and communicative acts to select for the interpretation and reconstruction of 'history' from the total social reality of the past....The starting point for historical interpretation may be the objective meaning context of the completed events, of the accomplished actions; but it may also be the subjective meaning context of a We in which every event was located. Hence, there can be a history of objective facts as well as a history of conduct, meaningful to the individual historical subject (Schutz, 1964).[1]

History as an observational science can get at its past only through the present and future. But scientific investigation does not end in its data; it begins with it. The outcome of science is a theory or working hypothesis, not so-called facts. It is not the recovery of the dream that we seek, but the interpretation thereof (Mead, 1964).[2]

The essay developed in this Chapter aims to grapple with each of these contrasting, but related points of view on history, including: (1) the problem of historiography and interpretation and (2) the uses to which historical interpretations are put.

The study and reconstruction of social history is highly dependent on the availability of accumulated, stored, and easily retrievable data that permit descriptions of events past in the unfolding of a group or society. However, these kinds of data such as medical records of veterans of military service are not always available nor easily accessible where they are in abundance, so far as histories of human groups are concerned.

The Limitations of Historiography

Village elders who may serve as oral historians, clay and stone etchings of nonliterate societies found through archeological excavations; microfiche, film, and electronic data processing of records in highly technological societies are some of the more obvious, durable, and frequently used instruments for developing, storing, and making retrievable historically valuable information. However, in any given social historical period, many events that occur during the life of a group may not be selected for recording and preservation by specialists who perform the function of developing archives.

Many factors help to determine the selection of a particular object, topic, record of achievement or other phenomenon for documentation and preservation for posterity: An event may mark an important point in the development of an individual, a family, a community, or an entire society. For example, the birth and death of family members are important events about which careful records commonly are kept in human groups. Marriage ceremonies, graduation from highly valued and socially defined role-training programs, such as colleges and universities; passage through puberty into womanhood and manhood, and other developments may be acknowledged by family and/or community celebrations, scarification rites, change in social status, funerals and a variety of other ceremonies which help mark the occurrence and accent the social significance of the event.

> Aside from the calculated acts of a record keeper, it should also be noted that "many 'documents' only accidentally preserved, and later recovered by others, are thought to be evidence of 'important points." It is not only the record keepers, but also the later audience, i.e., the 'historians,' who have a role in determining what is 'important.'[3]

The marking, dating, and storage of information about events such as birth, marriage, and death through photographic records, written notation, diaries, records of public speeches, books, etc. and the more recent advances in electronic data processing and storage systems make possible the simplification of coding and storage of large quantities of complex sets of data such as information on tax paying behavior, population change, occupational histories, and so on. Once collected and stored, these data become available for analysis by any member of a society who is permitted access to them and is familiar with the language and procedures by which it is coded, stored, made manipulable and amenable to analysis.

Frequently, a very important event in a group that is selected for special attention and dating such as child birth, is associated with a marked pleasure; another such as death, may be associated with discomfort for some or all members of a family and/or community. Usually, these events leave an indelible psychological effect on members of the community, whether or not formal records of the event are kept. For example, in nonliterate societies, an elderly member who may be a village chief may be charged with the responsibility of storing in his/her own memory details about important historical events such as deaths of very important persons who have affected group life.[4] The death of a shaman or a highly respected village leader, the premature death of the child of a chief, and military victories (or defeats) are especially likely to be recalled in sharp detail. Even in highly literate societies, both youth and elders seem to recall more accurately the birth and death of a family member than they recall the date of a marriage or when the newlyweds began to raise a family and establish their own household.[5] Life and death processes rank higher in systems of human values than mere change in the social and ecological distributions of persons in groups.[6] Thus, it seems reasonable to expect that events which rank low in a hierarchy of values are less likely to be recorded by indigenous historians and lay social scientists, and are less likely to be recalled explicitly in an oral historical interview than those events that (1) rank high in the system of values and (2) constitute radical disruptions in the health or life course of an individual, or a broad disruptive change in the society, such as war, a disease epidemic, or massive flood or fire that guts a place where a group makes its home. If these conclusions are correct, perhaps it was the tumultuous macroscopic effects and "mainstream" concern about the crash of the stock market in 1929 and the onset of the Great Depression in 1930 that effectively overshadowed the comparatively microscopic achievements of A.R. Johnston, a black man as it were, in his landmark election to the office of mayor of Miles Heights Village in 1929.

Ethnocentrism and the Development of Historical Records

There are other important factors that help to determine what and who gets selected for study by historians and social scientists. Included among these factors are the availability of trained investigators, economic support for social historical inquiry, and the gatekeeping practices represented by the values assigned by political, economic and literary decision makers, such as editors of archival materials, publishers, and panels of reviewers who screen proposals submitted as grant requests to funding agencies.[7] In general, these gatekeepers and others participate in constraining and/or inducing the development of historical and social science inquiry and documentation in selected directions, not necessarily those flowing from the imagination of research investigators.

Ethnocentrism is reflected by condescending attitudes, usually of one person or group toward another of a different class and/or ethnic group. Underlying such attitudes is a system of beliefs and values that suggests that all other ethnic groups when compared to that of the protagonist are socially and culturally inferior to the group in which he or she has membership.

Considering the time, energy requirements, and economic costs of social and historical research, ethnocentric gatekeepers of research funds and research investigators can be expected to argue, either deliberately or unwittingly, that the difficulties and costs associated with systematic research warrant assigning top priority to studies representing their own (the gatekeepers') ethnic interests. It is expected that secondary value would be assigned the prospective information that could be gained from detailed study of a social and cultural out-group, except when the prospective group is exotic and/or potentially dangerous to the society represented by the gatekeepers. If, for example, a white historian or social scientist belonged to a society that rewarded people for being white, while punishing and/or ignoring achievements of blacks, it would be reasonable to expect that the research career of the white historian would show a disproportionate interest (1) in studying and casting white people in a positive image in contrast to blacks[8] and (2) so far as blacks were selected for investigation, they would be studied as a negatively deviant or pathological variant of the idealized white social and cultural patterns.[9] Therefore, soul food, kinky hair, racially segregated housing, poor performance by blacks on standardized tests designed by whites-for-whites may all be read from a white ethnic point of view as symbolic of black pathology or cultural deviance rather than difference. References to behavior as deviant and/or pathological for any given social historical period can be understood as representations of the value premises and rules for behavior that help to structure the social perceptions of the research investigator rather than the full range of behavior and semantic nuances symbolized by the individual or group that the investigator describes.

In addition to the influence of ethnocentrism on the scholarly products of white historians and social scientists and the social historical exclusion of blacks from training in higher education, the absence of careful studies of black communities in part, can be accounted for by the dearth of blacks who have been permitted to undertake advanced studies in the disciplines of the social sciences.[10] Partly because of the growing ethnic consciousness of black people in the U.S., and the growing numbers of blacks trained since 1950 in social scientific and historical methods, increasing numbers of blacks in recent years have turned to reinterpreting the history of race relations and ethnic groups in the U.S. In large part, although not exclusively because of these factors revisionist histories by blacks have been aimed at determining the accuracy of descriptions and interpretations of social history proliferated and controlled by white social scientists and historians during the first two centuries of the U.S.[11]

One of the major tasks of black studies of history is to correct the stereotypical portrayals of blacks that have grown out of the ethnocentric studies of the Afro-American past. Another major purpose is to rewrite and carefully document histories and sociological studies of black communities that previously have been ignored, or paid scant attention in social histories of the U.S. Where there are few or no records of accomplished events, nor photographic plates or other kinds of materials which could document social historical events, alternative techniques of data collection and record development must be cultivated.

Oral Accounts of Historical Events

Oral historical documentation through systematically collected life history interviews constitute one useful way of gaining insight into the history and social organization of a community such as "Old Miles Heights" and developing manipulable data that otherwise would be lost with the death of the surviving griots, oracles and other oral historians. Secondly, these kinds of data help to make possible comparative sociological and ethnographic studies of different groups within and between different sociotemporal periods, as well as communities or residential settings held constant in time. The recent study by Gwalthney[12] that is aptly subtitled, "a self-portrait of Black America" is an anthropological account of a small black community based primarily on analyses of oral historical materials. Meyerhoff and Simic's studies of Life's Careers[13] and Kennedy's study of "Black Family Relations in a Southern Community"[14] also make important contributions in this area. In the absence of these kinds of studies, knowledge of history, culture and social organization would be more conjectural and speculative than it currently stands.

In an oral historical interview, the research investigator may encounter We- or They-relations as the interactional context in which the interview unfolds.[15] We-relations are most likely to be present when the investigator interviews a member of his or her family, an old friend, or someone similarly close whom he or she has known on intimate terms.

As pointed out at the opening of Chapter I, my earliest exposure to oral historical contents about the Village occurred through We-relations focused on folktales told by my father and other old-timers in THE VILLAGE. It is noteworthy that We-relations played significant parts in the interactional contexts of the studies by Gwalthney and Kennedy cited above.

In contrast to We-relations, They-relations are constituted by the investigator interacting with a virtual stranger, or whose focus is upon the past behavior of strangers with whom the investigator shared little or no common culture.[16] According to Schutz, the more anonymous the interaction partner, for example in They-relations when compared to We-relations, the more "objectively" must the investigator (interviewer) use the "sign-systems" through which he or she attempts to communicate with the informant.[17] Increased objectivity or the concretization of referents is needed to minimize erroneous messages and misunderstanding between the investigator and the informant (interviewee). One final distinction made by Schutz is stated as follows: "I cannot presuppose, for example, that my partner in a They-relation will grasp a nuance of a word or that he will place a statement of mine in the proper context unless I explicitly and 'objectively' refer to that context. The direct evidence that I have been understood, which I have if my partner is present in the community of space and time, is lacking in a They-relation."[18]

The primary interviews conducted in this study were set within the context of We-relations. This was made possible by the fact that the investigator was born and reared in THE

VILLAGE. As such, the understanding shown in this study of the life of THE VILLAGE is a contribution that grew in part out of the We-relations of the investigator with old-time residents of THE VILLAGE.

In the study of THE VILLAGE, oral history meant a reconstruction of events past through in-depth interviews focused upon the lived-experiences of the informant and/or his/her perception and recall of major and minor events that occurred in the development of another individual or group within a relatively definite and dateable period.[19] The focus of inquiry through oral accounts may be events so far past that probing into the deepest recesses of the memory of the interviewee is required. For example, in a community study, the ideal interviewee is someone who has lived before, during, and after the social historical period selected for study. This kind of interviewee can help to provide the greatest possible detail about antecedent social, political, economic, psychological and other factors related to the particular period as well as the specific factors selected for detailed analysis.

Oral historical interviews also permit gaining insight into motivating forces behind the behaviors of the individual or group selected for study. This means that the earlier the historical period selected for description and analysis, the older must be the interviewee or oral historian as measured in chronological years. This requirement is imposed by the ideal that persons selected for oral historical interviews should have lived through the sociotemporal period and behavior setting selected for study.

Unlike the definitions of oral history set forth by Seldon and Pappworth in *By Word of Mouth*,[20] the Library of Congress,[21] and the *Encyclopedia of Library and Information Science*,[22] the conception of oral history advanced in this study is focused more concisely as follows: (1) the aim is the reconstruction of events past (2) that occurred within a relatively definite or dateable period, and (3) are associated with the lived-experiences of the informant (interviewee) or his/her recall of major and minor events that have occurred in the development of another individual or group. By contrast, Seldon and Pappworth (1983) loosely defined oral history as "information transmitted orally, in a personal exchange, of a kind likely to be of historical or long term value."[23] This definition is inadequate because it does not concisely distinquish the oral historical interview from any other type, nor does it focus on events past with dateable periods. Similar criticism can be made of the Library of Congress' conception that defines oral history as a "record of information gathered in oral form usually on tape, as the result of a planned interview"[24] and the *Encyclopedia of Library and Information Science* that conceives "oral history as primary source material obtained by recording the spoken words--generally by means of planned, tape recorded interviews of persons deemed to harbor hitherto unavailable information worth preserving."[25] Each of the latter definitions seems to have as a primary concern the selection and recording of information worth preserving, a consequence of which is the development of historical records. This kind of record can be conceived as "oral historical" only in the sense that the original source of information occurred through a personal or oral interview, the content of which subsequently was recorded and stored, effectively establishing these records as documents that may be retreived and used by posterity to conduct research on the world(s) of their predecessors. By contrast, the conception and method of oral historical data collected in the study of THE VILLAGE focused at the outset through a carefully planned schedule of interview questions on events past, not the present in process of becoming past.

While it seems reasonable to expect that living through a sociotemporal period is most favorable to density of memory for events of that period, this requirement may not be practical in all uses of life history interviews. Nor does this mean that other persons with secondary information and/or a history of indirect experiences with the objects of analysis cannot provide useful information. It does mean that the information provided by secondary and tertiary sources is more likely to be conjectural and less reliable when compared to interviews of persons who lived through the sociotemporal period and behavior setting selected for study.[26] The ability to recall accurately and articulate clearly details about events past is perhaps the most troublesome problem with oral historical interviews.

Achieving a high degree of objectivity in this study was attempted by cross-validating each interview with one or more other interviews of old-timers in the same birth cohort. Secondly, through the use of archival materials and other authoritative references on various periods and facets of THE VILLAGE, the accuracy of the findings of this study was enhanced.

Facilitating Recall in the Study of Behavior in a Community Setting

Achieving accurate and detailed recall of events has a considerable bearing on the reliability of accounts based upon oral historical interviews. Unlike oral historical research, interviews conducted through cross-sectional survey research commonly place the focus of the investigator's attention on the collection of data through fixed formats for responses to standardized questions.[27] The fixed formats are intended to guide the presentation of questions and responses theoretically, to minimize the risk of interviewer and questionnaire bias and the time and costs in coding and preparing data for quantitative analyses.

Oral historical interviews which are normally in-depth with open ended response formats (the kind used in this study) are less structured. The investigator may ask the interviewee to focus on a specific topic or event rather than specific questions about it. Interaction between the interviewer and the interviewee may then be focused on inquiry through conversation about the topic or event in response to which the interviewee is permitted to range widely, for example through "free association" over a variety of impressions that he/she may reveal about the topic of discussion. The investigator may choose to interrupt or ask questions to increase his or her chances of collecting as a minimum the kind of detail that he or she wants in the interview protocol about the object of analysis.

Uses of interview techniques to collect from elderly people oral historical data about individual and group experiences do not always lend themselves to the rigorous requirements of structured questionnaires and interview techniques that may be used or emphasized in survey research. Open ended interviews may be suitable in studies requiring elderly people as informants for the purpose of developing life history data with a focus on community description and analysis. However, in addition to poor memory, the informant of advanced age may be impaired in other ways that may interfere with data collection.

As temporal distance increases between the point in time at which an event occurred and the point when an interviewer requires recall of details about the event, there is a risk of decreasing memory of specific details about the event.[28] A variety of factors seems to be associated with decreasing ability to recall details about events in the distant past.

Chronic brain syndrome that increasingly is likely with advancing age after 40, is one of the factors most frequently cited as a determinant of loss of recall. However, the arguments for this proposition are questionable. There is an implicit assumption that memory for details and youthfulness are related. In other words, the younger a person, as measured by chronological years of age, the sharper is his or her memory for details about events past, holding constant the date of the event about which each cohort of interviewees is asked to give detailed information. Conversely, it is implied that growing old is negatively associated with the ability to exercise recall. Clearly, however, it is brain deterioration and other factors, not age as such, that is the menace of memory with advancing age.[29] Apoplexy (or stroke), atherosclerosis (or hardening of the arteries), Alzheimer's disease and other cerebrovascular disorders can also interfere with processes of memory and other functions of the central nervous system.

The elderly interviewee may be hard of hearing and, as a result, may require that complex survey questions be simplified or even visually illustrated. For example, photographs of people or sketches of places may be needed to facilitate recall about events that occurred many decades earlier in his/her lifetime. Maps depicting earlier patterns of the geography of a community, photo reproductions of old houses, and newspaper clippings about events past were used in this study of THE VILLAGE. Similar objects were used to induce recall in previous research by Watson,[30] on growing old in the black belt of the United States, and by Dollard,[31] in *Class and Caste In A Southern Town*.

The elderly interviewee may be blind and require that questions initially focused by the interviewer on visually experiential phenomena be restated in terms of the interviewee's functioning senses, previous We-relations shared in his or her biographical past, and other referents that permit him or her to make a meaningful response.

In an historical and ethnographic study of a small community such as THE VILLAGE about which finely detailed reports are highly desirable but few documentary materials are available, it may be wise to dispense with highly structured formal interview schedules that suggest *a priori* closure on responses to the range of pertinent questions that may be asked informants. Instead, it may be advisable to use each interview protocol and substantive response(s) thereto, and/or the content of an interview developed through free association as guides to planning subsequent and more in-depth interviews of the same person, or the next interviewee.[32] Accurate and detailed descriptions of remembered and/or observable events are especially favorable to developing data sets for use in determining the reliability of claims made by other interviewees about statements of fact pertaining to the same events, points in time, and details about behavior settings and related events in the history of a community. These uses of interviews in social science field research are especially desirable when the investigator is seeking in-depth information from several different people about a common object or setting such as the black community selected for study in this research.

Conclusions

This chapter examined the thesis that social history is a socially constructed account of accomplished events and/or event sequences. It was reaffirmed, as many social scientists did many times before, that the substance of social historical facts does not reside merely in the nature of the object(s) of analysis, as for example, the acts of the combatants of the First or Second World Wars or the economic developments of the Depression of the 1930s. Instead, as social and historical facts, perceptions and accounts of events past, such as wars, the mayoralty of Arthur R. Johnston, and economic depression are highly structured by the belief systems of scientists, including paradigms prevailing in social science thought, and the taken-for-granted beliefs and values embedded in the fabric of society in which the historian or social scientist lives and adjusts as he or she performs the investigative and interpretative acts of historical analysis. It is in this sense that historical facts are interpretative.[33]

This chapter showed that historical and sociological research are fraught with many methodological problems that have considerable bearing on the substance and reliability of findings ultimately produced. Included among them are: (1) Value intrusion in the selection or omission of objects of analysis. For example, a sense of status parity and common fate among some women and blacks may lead feminists to study womens' issues and blacks to show a predominant interest in black issues, partly due to their respective value premises about the importance of actual and/or idealized feminist movements, on the one hand, and black social movements on the other; or the corresponding beliefs among some members of each group that women are best suited to do unbiased research on women, and blacks on blacks. (2) The unwavering commitment of the investigator to unearth every possible detail that might help to illuminate his/her object of analysis, as opposed to ending an investigation after securing the results of one test or a series of inconclusive observations. (3) The credibility of sources of information, such as informants and printed records, as well as questionnaires and interview schedules designed to elicit information about events past. (4) The relative freedom of the investigator(s) and informant(s) from bias in the definition of evidence and selection of documentation. (5) The exercise of carefully designed systematic procedures for executing the overall research project. (6) Meticulous interpretation of findings.

At various points in time and circumstances associated with the research on THE VILLAGE each of these problems emerged and, in turn, was resolved during the course of the study. In this chapter on the social construction of social history, the primary focus was on the first four problems listed. The question of the possibility of value intrusion in the choice of one or omission of another object of analysis grew out of the omission of attention to Arthur R. Johnston in three recent books on the history of blacks in Cleveland and/or Ohio. As documented in Chapter 3 of this book, Johnston was the first black mayor of a predominantly white incorporated village in the history of Ohio. Moreover, Johnston achieved this distinction some 38 years before the landmark victory of Carl Stokes, whose election to the Office of Mayor of Cleveland, Ohio in 1967 distinguished him as the first black mayor of a major city in the United States. It should be noted, however, that the concern in this chapter was not the distinction between the achievements of Johnston and Stokes, but the social construction of the omission, or "ignorance," to borrow a term from Moore and Tumin,[34] of Johnston in the historical records of blacks in the political history of Ohio.

Several propositions were advanced that could help to account for the constraining effects of social factors on the construction of social history. Included among them were (1) class, sex and ethnic biases which may deliberately or unwittingly induce a preference to focus ethnocentrically on matters of culture class interests rather than universal issues; (2)

political, economic and professional pressures on historians and social scientists may induce studies of certain topics or sociotemporal events while ignoring others. For example, state constraints represented by federal requests for fundable research proposals that specify what the government will and will not fund may indirectly but effectively shape the substantive development of documentary materials for decades. This is especially likely in a society like the U.S. where in 1980, 65 percent of all social science research was funded by the federal government. The U.S. is also a society where universities and private research firms are increasingly giving preferential treatment to faculty and investigators who are successful in grant development; and (3) where technical writers, librarians, griots and others who are trusted to protect socially important documents play significant roles in the social construction of social histories, whether they act consciously or unwittingly in the interest of posterity.

Finally, this chapter closed with a discussion of uses and limitations of oral accounts of historical events as a technique of documenting the past. Oral histories, the term popularly used to refer to this technique, are especially useful for documenting events and event sequences about places, people and periods, such as THE VILLAGE during the 1920s, about which our predecessors left no formal records except scattered newspaper clippings. However, because the contemporary development of oral accounts is dependent largely on elderly informants, especially if the research focus is on their lived experiences, the risk of information loss through death of informants before interviews can be completed is great. The more ancient the historical period and the older the informant required to produce an account, the more likely the prospective informant(s) will be lost or unavailable due to age-related risks of chronic, debilitating illness and mortality. This technique is limited also with advancing age after 60 by the risks of cognitive disorientation for space and time and associated decrements in the ability of informants to recall accurately events past. In spite of these limitations and others, however, oral accounts of historical events are useful ways of (1) supplementing information gained from research carried out through the use of other more traditional historical materials such as archives, and (2) filling information gaps in the historical record about places, people, events, and periods that were neglected and undocumented by our predecessors.

The conduct of careful historical and sociological research is not a "mid-summer nights dream." The fruits of these kinds of labors can be bountiful and enlightening, as were the results of this study of THE VILLAGE. But the intellectual tasks and commitment to meticulous conscientious inquiry are momentous, as aptly stated by Schutz in the quotation that opened this chapter. Nevertheless, it is hoped that this study of THE VILLAGE has deepened our understanding of the social history of black Americans in Ohio and problems in the social construction of history in general.

Appendix A

KEY LIBRARY, ARCHIVAL, AND ORAL HISTORICAL RESOURCES FOR THIS STUDY

As noted in the acknowledgements, there were numerous individuals, families and family records, and organized support groups that helped to make this study and written record possible. The libraries and archives included the following: The Western Reserve Historical Society in Cleveland, Ohio where, with the able guidance of Mrs. Olivia Martin, I was first exposed in 1970 to newspaper clippings on A. R. Johnston. The History Division of the main branch of the Cleveland Public Library was also helpful through its extensive file of newspaper clippings and microfilms of the Cleveland Press, Plain Dealer, and the Call and Post on old Miles Heights from 1925-1978. Other helpful resources included the Ernie Bohn Papers, Special Collections of the Freiberger Library of Case Western Reserve University, Cleveland, Ohio. The Bohn papers were helpful in tracing patterns of housing and transportation developments in Cleveland. Mrs. Mary Tekavec of Alta House of the Greater Cleveland Federation of settlements was helpful during my attempt to locate sources on the history of Italian migration and settlement in the Cleveland metropolitan area, and THE VILLAGE, in particular.

Other important sources of information were the staff of the Regional Transit Authority of Cleveland, Ohio; the Lee-Harvard and the East Cleveland Branches of the Cleveland Public Library System; the Atlanta University Center Robert W. Woodruff Library; the Public Relations Officer of the

Cuyahoga County Metropolitan Housing Authority; the Cleveland and Warrensville Heights Boards of Education; the American Committee on Italian Immigration, Richmond Heights, Ohio; and the German Cultural Society of Cleveland in Berea, Ohio.

I am especially grateful to members of the following families for permitting me to glimpse through their eyes and oral historical interviews the life-styles of the people of old Miles Heights and THE VILLAGERS, in particular.

Sources of Oral Historical Interviews

The Johnston Family

    Constance Parton
    Leola Fantroy

The Gary Family

    James Gary, Jr.
    (deceased)

The Watson Family

    Lovest Lee Watson
    (deceased)
    Marjorie C. Williford
     Watson
    Ralph Watson
    Sanford E. Watson

The Murray Family

    Hobart Murray

The Oatman Family

    Martha Oatman
    (deceased)
    Sallie May Watson-
    Oatman (deceased)
    Frank Oatman

The Hall Family

    Mildred Hall

THE VILLAGE 155

The Watson Family Continued

>Marlene L. Watson (Leverette)
>Mary Lou Watson (deceased)

The Williford Family

>Marjorie Williford Watson
>Ruth Williford Barry
>Herleen Williford

The Anthony Family

>William Anthony
>Walter Anthony

The Smith Family

>Earl Smith

The Gresham Family

>Crandell Gresham
>Beatrice (Bee) Gresham
>Arzell Gresham
>Johnell Gresham

The Brooks Family

>Paul Brooks
>Gail Brooks
>Nate Brooks

The Crosby Family

>Addie Crosby-Jackson
>Kathleen Crosby

The Lewis Family

>Joe Nathan Lewis
>Mary Lewis Robinson

The Garnett Family

>Robert O. Garnett

The Robinson Family

>Harvey Lee Robinson

The Stewart Family

>Scherrie Stewart

The Withers Family

Ronald Withers

Other Sources of Data

Rev. J. D. Smith
Former Associate Pastor
Canaan Missionary Baptist
Church and former resident
of THE VILLAGE

Rev. Wilbert E. Jackson
Pastor
Canaan Missionary Baptist
Church and former resident of THE VILLAGE

"Bubbie" Lewis, former resident of THE VILLAGE

Through a telephone interview with Wandell Leverette, Lewis revealed that his family owned and operated a drugstore in the "Seville Homes" Shopping Center from 1948-1951. The proprietor was Lorenzo Lewis, Sr. (wife's name was Alice).

Mary Penn, June 28, 1984

Telephone interview about former Italians who resided in THE VILLAGE. Mrs. Penn is a former resident of THE VILLAGE.

ENDNOTES

Foreword

[1] Ferdinand Tonnies, *Community and Society: Gemeinschaft and Gesselschaft*. Charles P. Loomis, Ed. East Lansing, Michigan: Michigan State University Press, **1957**.

[2] Emile Durkheim, *The Division of Labor in Society*. New York: Free Press of Glencoe, **1964**.

[3] Gerald D. Suttles, *The Social Order of the Slum: Ethnicity and Territory in the Inner City*. Chicago: University of Chicago Press, **1968**.

[4] Nelson W. Polsby, *Community Power and Political Theory*. New Haven, Connecticut: Yale University Press, **1980**.

[5] Herbert J. Gans, *The Urban Villagers*. New York: Free Press of Glencoe, **1965**.

[6] James E. Blackwell, *The Black Community: Diversity and Unity*, 2nd Edition, New York: Harper and Row, **1985**.

[7] Robert S. Lynd and Helen M. Lynd, *Middletown: A Study in American Culture*. New York: Harcourt, Brace, **1929**.

Preface

[1] W. E. B. Dubois, "The Study of the Negro Problem." (Speech delivered by Dubois before the American Academy of Political and Social Science November 19, 1897). Reprinted in Lester, Julius, Ed., *The Seventh Son, I: The Thought and Writings of W. E. B. Dubois.* New York: Random House, **1971**, p. 229.

[2] Harry A. Ploski and James Williams, Eds., *The Negro Almanac: A Reference Work on the Afro-American.* Fourth Edition. New York: John Wiley and Sons, **1983**, p. 404.

[3] Dwight W. Hoover, "Black History," p. 48. In Martin Ballard, ed., *New Movements in the Study and Teaching of History.* Bloomington and London: Indiana University Press, **1970**.

[4] Beatrice Whiting and John Whiting, "Methods for Observing and Recording Behavior," pp. 282-315. In Raoul Naroll and Ronald Cohen, eds. *A Handbook of Method in Cultural Anthropology.* Garden City, N.Y.: The Natural History Press, **1970**. I am also grateful for correspondence with Robert Kastenbaum and his writing about Barbara Meyerhoff's uses of data on story telling that helped to reinforce the importance of this technique of social and cultural analysis.

[5] Allison Davis, Burleigh B. Gardner, and Mary R. Gardner, *Deep South.* Chicago: The University of Chicago Press, **1941**. Also see Charles S. Johnson, *Growing up in the*

Black Belt: Negro Youth in the Rural South. New York: Schocken Books, **1941**.

[6]Zora Neal Hurston, *Tell My Horse.* Turtle Island: The Turtle Island Foundation, **1983**.

[7]Langston Hughes and Arna Bontemps, eds., *The Book of Negro Folklore.* New York: Dodd, Mead and Company, **1983**.

[8]Theodore R. Kennedy, *You Gotta Deal With It.* New York: Oxford University Press, **1980**.

[9]John Langston Gwalthney, *Drylongso: A Self-Portrait of Black America .* New York: Vintage Books, **1981**.

[10]Shepard Krech, III, *Praise The Bridge That Carries You Over: The Life of Joseph L. Sutton.* Cambridge, MA: Schenkman Publishing Co., **1981**.

[11]Josef Haekel, "Source Criticism in Anthropology," pp. 147-164. In Raoul Naroll and Ronald Cohen, eds., *A Handbook of Method in Cultural Anthropology.* Garden City, New York: The Natural History Press, **1970**. Also see Louis Wirth, *The Ghetto.* Chicago: University of Chicago Press, **1956**, pp. 8-10, 282-284.

[12]Clifford Geertz, *The Interpretation of Cultures.* New York: Basic Books, **1973**. Although my study and writing on THE VILLAGE may have only scratched the surface of the approach to "thick description" described by Geertz in chap-

ter one of *The Interpretation of Cultures*, his discussion nevertheless guided my approach to inquire in this study.

Interfaces of Autobiography and Social History

[1] Alfred Schutz, "The World of Predecessors and the Problem of History," p. 8. In Alfred Schutz, *Collected Papers, II: Studies in Social Theory* (Ed. and Introduced by Arvid Brodersen). The Hague, Netherlands: Martinus Nijhoff, **1964**, pp. 58-59.

[2] St. Clair Drake and Horace R. Cayton, *Black Metropolis: A Study of Negro Life In A Northern City*. New York: Harper and Row, **1962**, p. 395.

[3] LeRoi Jones, *Blues People*. New York: William Morrow Company, **1966**, pp. 95-97.

[4] See for example Howard Schuman, et al, *Racial Attitudes In America: Trends and Interpretations*. Cambridge, Massachusetts: Harvard University Press, **1985**, pp. 77-135; and Drake and Cayton, op. cit., pp. 716-767.

[5] Ida Wells-Barnett, *On Lynchings*. New York: Arno Press and The New York Times, **1969**.

[6] For previous discussions of related issues, see Gunnar Myrdal, *Objectivity in Social Research*, New York: Pantheon Books, **1969**; Robert K. Merton, Notes on Problem-Finding in Sociology, pp. ix-xxxiv. In Robert K. Merton, Leonard Broom and Leonard S. Cottrell, Jr., *Sociology Today, Vol. I:*

Problems and Prospects. New York: Harper Torchbooks, **1959**.

[7]For related discussions see Irving Louis Horowitz, "The Sociology Textbook: The Treatment of Conflict in American Sociological Literature." *International Social Science Council Information*, 11, 1 (February-August, 1972): 51-63; Karl Mannheim, *Ideology and Utopia.* New York: Harcourt, Brace & World, Inc., 1936. Thomas S. Kuhn, *The Structure of Scientific Revolutions*, 2nd edition. Chicago: University of Chicago Press, **1970**.

[8]Schutz, op. cit., pp. 61-62.

[9]Ibid.

[10]Peter L. Berger and Thomas Luckman, *The Social Construction of Reality: A Treatise in the Sociology of Knowledge.* New York: Anchor Books, 1966. Also see "The Sociological Significance of the Ghetto," especially pages 287-289 in Louis Wirth, *The Ghetto.* Chicago: University of Chicago Press, **1956**.

[11]Max Weber, *The Methodology of the Social Sciences* (Translated and Edited by E. A. Shils and H. A. Finch). New York: The Free Press, **1949**, p. 173.

[12]Mannheim, op. cit., pp. 102-103.

[13]George Herbert Mead, "Time," pp. 328-341. In Anselm Strauss, ed., *George Herbert Mead: On Social Psychology.* Chicago: University of Chicago Press, **1964**, p. 329.

¹⁴For another point of view, see Goffman's interpretation of the essay by William James on "The Perception of Reality" in which Goffman noted that:

The important thing about reality is our sense of its realness in contrast to our feeling that some things lack this quality. One can then ask under what conditions such a feeling is generated, and this question speaks to a small, manageable problem having to do with the camera and not what it is the camera takes pictures of.

See E. Goffman on *Frame Analysis.* New York: Harper and Row, **1974**, p. 2.

Everybody Was Family

¹"Pope, In Farewell, Tells New Yorkers 'A City Needs A Soul.'" *The New York Times,* Thursday (Late City Edition), October 4, **1979**, p. 1.

²Addie Crosby-Jackson, early settler. Oral historical interview in her home in THE VILLAGE, March 6, 1984.

³Johnell Gresham, son of an early settler. Oral historical interview, Cleveland, Ohio, December 29, 1985.

⁴Information collected through an interview with a former member of a border family and who is currently an archival reader, Western Reserve Historical Society. This informant did not want to be identified by name.

THE VILLAGE

[5] Lovest Lee Watson, early settler. Oral historical interview, June 25, 1984.

[6] Walter Anthony, son of an early settler. Oral historical interview on December 26, 1983. This account, given by Walter Anthony, was confirmed by William Anthony, an early settler and cousin of Walter, oral historical interview, December 27, 1983.

[7] Walter Anthony, oral historical interview, November 23, 1984. This account was corroborated on November 23, 1984 in a separate interview with Lovest Lee Watson, an early settler who was familiar with the work of the Anthony family.

[8] Lovest Lee Watson, early settler. Oral historical interview, December 25, 1983.

[9] Ibid.

[10] John C. Ferguson, History of Saint Paul Methodist Church. Cleveland, Ohio, 1953 (unpublished document made available for this study by Mrs. Mildred Hall, Church Historian and resident of THE VILLAGE, December 1983).

[11] William Anthony, an early settler. Oral historical interview at the home of Mrs. Mildred Hall, December 23, 1983. This account was also documented through an oral historical interview with Lovest L. Watson, op. cit., 1983.

[12] *The Cleveland Press*, "She Recalls the Old Days in Miles Heights," Community News, Thursday, December 4, 1969, p. G-1.

[13] Ibid.

[14] Walter Anthony, op. cit., **1984**.

[15] Watson, op. cit., December 23, 1983.

[16] Kenneth L. Kusmer, *A Ghetto Takes Shape: Black Cleveland, 1870-1930*. Urbana, Illinois: University of Illinois Press, **1976**.

[17] Andrew Billingsley, *Black Families in White America*. Englewood Cliffs, New Jersey: Prentice Hall, Inc., **1968**, p. 65.

[18] Gresham, op. cit.

[19] Lovest Lee Watson, op. cit., June 25, 1984.

[20] Niles Carpenter, "Nationality, Color, and Economic Opportunity in the City of Buffalo." *University of Buffalo Studies* 5, June, 1927: 45-194.

[21] Billingsley, op. cit., p. 65.

[22] Howard Schuman, Charlotte Steeh, and Lawrence Bobo. *Racial Attitudes In America: Trends and Interpretations*. Cambridge, Massachusetts: Harvard University Press, **1985**, p. 195.

[23] Constance Parton, Oral historical interview, December 23, 1983.

[24] Ibid.; this observation was later corroborated by Lovest Lee Watson, op. cit., June 25, 1984.

[25] Sanford Watson, oldest living son of an early settler. Oral historical interview March 10, 1984. This account was later corroborated by Wandell J. Leverette (former President of the Nucleus, 1983), June 23, 1984.

[26] Gresham, op. cit.

[27] Ibid.

[28] Scherrie Stewart, current resident of THE VILLAGE. Oral historical interview, March 10, 1984.

[29] Ibid. Stewart was a co-organizer of the first reunion/picnic.

[30] Joe Nathan Lewis, son of an early settler. Oral historical interview, Cleveland, Ohio, December 29, 1985.

[31] Stewart, op. cit.

[32] Gresham, op. cit.

[33] Lewis, op. cit.

[34] Ibid. This account was corroborated by Arzell Gresham, eldest son of an early settler. Oral historical interview, Cleveland, Ohio, December 29, 1985.

[35] Arthur J. Vidich and Joseph Bensman. *Small Town in Mass Society: Class, Power, and Religion in a Rural Community.* New York: Anchor, **1960**.

[36] Ibid., pp. 9-10, 80.

[37] James E. Blackwell, *The Black Community - Diversity & Unity.* New York: Harper and Row, **1985**, p. xii.

[38] Johnell Gresham, op. cit.

[39] Nathan Brooks, son of an early settler. Oral historical interview at his home in THE VILLAGE, December 30, 1985.

[40] Arzell Gresham, oldest son of an early settler. Oral historical interview, Cleveland, Ohio, December 29, 1985.

[41] Vidich and Bensman, op. cit., p. 30.

[42] Brooks, op. cit.

[43] Ibid.

[44] Alwyn Barr, *Black Texas: History of Negroes in Texas, 1528-1971.* Austin, Texas: Jenkins Publishing Company, **1973**, p. 169.

[45] Ibid.

[46] Ibid.

⁴⁷Ibid.

⁴⁸Ibid.

Power and Politics

¹*Cleveland Plain Dealer*, "A. R. Johnston, County's First Negro Mayor, is Dead at 65." Thursday, April 25, 1957, p. 13.

²James Gary, Jr., son of an early settler. Oral historical interview, Cleveland, Ohio, June 1, 1974.

³Carter G. Woodson, *The History of the Negro Church*. Washington, DC: The Associated Publishers, 1985, p. 213.

⁴*Cleveland Plain Dealer*, op. cit. Acknowledgement is made also of the recently published study by Russel H. Davis on *Black Americans in Cleveland*, Washington, D.C.: Associated Publishers, **1972**, not because it helps to document the analysis presented in this chapter, nor the overall study of THE VILLAGE, but because it pretends to be a thorough coverage of black history in Cleveland from 1796-1969. In fact, Davis' study hardly acknowledges the presence of old Miles Heights and reports nothing at all about the history of blacks in Miles Heights village except for a five word reference to "the old Miles Heights area" (p. 329). With so little said, the reader with a keen interest in the social history of blacks in Cleveland can hardly gain much insight from Davis. The book is better read for its value as a chronicle of achievements of selected individuals and interest groups and

of population change among blacks rather than a study of blacks, qua blacks, in the history of Cleveland.

[5] Bill Ingram, "Miles Heights was Really Wild Town." Cleveland Press, April 4, 1969, p. B-12.

[6] While the Johnston daughters, Constance Parton and Leola Fantroy, specified Black River, Jamaica as A. R. Johnston's birthplace, a handwritten resume composed and left by Johnston (dated 1946) identified Southfield, Jamaica as his birthplace. Since the resume was Johnston's personal deposition, it was used as the authoritative source on his birthplace. The handwritten resume cited in this footnote was made available to me by Constance Parton, in her home on November 23, 1984.

[7] Ibid.

[8] A handwritten resume of Arthur R. Johnston, made available to me by Constance Parton, November 23, 1984.

[9] *Cleveland Call and Post*, Thursday, October 12, 1939, p. 3. By the time of the final writing of this project, no sources of information were available, including Mrs. Constance Parton, Mrs. Leola Fantroy, nor any other sources that specified where A. R. Johnston received his primary and secondary school education.

[10] Constance Parton, oldest daughter of A. R. Johnston, oral historical interview, April, 1976. Leola Fantroy, the second daughter born to Arthur R. and Annabell Johnston, must also be acknowledged for interviews on the Johnston's

family life. It should be noted that neither of Johnston's daughters, nor any other available sources, were able to specify whether A. R. Johnston moved to Cleveland alone or with his parents in 1913.

[11]Constance Parton. Oral historical interview at her home in THE VILLAGE, December 17, 1984.

[12]Constance Parton, oral historical interview at her home in THE VILLAGE, November 23, 1984.

[13]Naturalization papers of Arthur R. Johnston, made available by Constance Parton, December 7, 1984.

[14]*Cleveland Call and Post*, "Ex-Mayor of Miles Heights Buried." Saturday, May 4, 1957, p. 6-A. Also see the Cleveland Press, "She Recalls the Old Days in Miles Heights." *Community News,* Special section of *The Cleveland Press;* Thursday, December 4, 1969, p. G-1.

[15]Constance Parton, oral historical interview on November 23, 1984.

[16]Ibid. Also see the Cleveland Press, op. cit., "She Recalls the Old Days in Miles Heights," p. G-1.

[17]Constance Parton, oral historical interview, at her home in THE VILLAGE, April 1976.

[18]Greater Cleveland: A Bulletin On Public Business by the Citizens League, Volume V, No. 28 (April 10, 1930): 139-144.

[19]Ibid.

[20]Ibid., p. 140.

[21]*Cleveland Plain Dealer*, January 29, 1929.

[22]Gary, op. cit.

[23]Sharon M. Watson, "The Second Time Around: A Profile of Black Mayoral Reelection Campaigns." *Phylon* 45, 3 (September, 1984): 165-178.

[24]Ibid., p. 172.

[25]James E. Blackwell, *The Black Community: Unity and Diversity.* New York: Harper, **1985**, p. 244.

[26]Gary, op. cit.

[27]Robert Blauner, "Internal Colonialism and Ghetto Revolt." *Social Problems* 16 (Spring, 1969): 393-408.

[28]Constance Parton, oral historical interview, November 23, 1984.

[29]James E. Blackwell and Marie Haug, "Relations Between Black Bosses and Black Workers." *The Black Scholar*, 4 (January, 1973): 36-43.

[30]*Cleveland Plain Dealer*, June 9, 1931.

[31]*Cleveland Press*, op. cit., "She Recalls the Old Days," p. G-1.

[32]*Greater Cleveland*, op. cit., p. 139.

[33]*Cleveland Plain Dealer*, "Miles Heights is Annexed By City." March 29, 1932, p. 6.

[34]*Cleveland Plain Dealer*, "Miles Sanitation Imperils Health." April 27, 1932, p. 2.

[35]*Cleveland Plain Dealer*, op. cit., "Miles Heights is Annexed," p. 6.

[36]Ibid., p. 6.

[37]Ibid.

[38]Ibid.

[39]Ibid.

[40]Ibid.

[41]Kathleen Crosby, oral historical interview, Cleveland, Ohio, March 4, 1984.

[42]*Cleveland Plain Dealer*, op. cit., "Miles Heights is Annexed, p. 6.

[43]*Cleveland Press*. "Fight to Open Miles Heights School October 5." September 25, 1931, p. 16.

[44] *Cleveland Plain Dealer*, "Miles Heights, Board Deadlocked; Schools Will Not Be Opened." October 2, 1931, p. 17.

[45] Ibid. Also see the *Cleveland Plain Dealer*, "Miles Heights With School Shut, Votes Teachers' Back Pay." October 13, 1931, p. 10.

[46] *Cleveland Plain Dealer*, "Schools Get Hope at Miles Heights." September 23, 1931, p. 4.

[47] *Cleveland Plain Dealer*, op. cit., "Miles Heights With Schools Shut, p. 10.

[48] Ibid.; also claimed by Lovest Lee Watson, early settler, oral historical interview, Cleveland, Ohio, March, 1976.

[49] *Cleveland Plain Dealer*, op. cit., "Miles Heights With Schools Shut," p. 10. Also see the *Cleveland Plain Dealer*, "Seek State's Help to Start Schools in Miles Heights." September 29, 1931.

[50] Ibid., *Cleveland Plain Dealer*, "Seek State's Help to Start Schools in Miles Heights."

[51] *Cleveland Plain Dealer*, op. cit., "Schools Get Hope at Miles Heights," p. 4.

[52] *Cleveland Plain Dealer*, op. cit., "Miles Heights Board Deadlocked," p. 17.

[53] *Cleveland Plain Dealer,* op. cit., "Miles Heights is Annexed," p. 6.

[54] *Cleveland Plain Dealer,* "Miles Sanitation Imperils Health," p. 2.

[55] Ibid.

[56] Gary, op. cit.

[57] *Cleveland Plain Dealer,* op. cit., "Miles Heights is Annexed by City," p. 6.

[58] *Cleveland Plain Dealer,* "Miles Schools Unite With City in 10 Days." April 1, 1932, p. 8.

[59] *Cleveland Plain Dealer,* op. cit. "Arthur R. Johnston, County's First Negro Mayor," p. 13.

[60] *Cleveland Call and Post,* "Governor Bricker Appoints Race Man to Tax Division," Thursday, October 12, 1939, p. 3.

[61] Mrs. Annabell Johnston died December 8, 1970. Surviving in 1988 are the Johnston's two daughters, Mrs. Constance Parton and Mrs. Leola B. Fantroy, six grandchildren, and seven great grandchildren.

Health, Illness, and Coping with Adversity

[1] Johnell Gresham, son of early settler. Oral historical interview, Cleveland, Ohio, December 29, 1985.

[2] Mary Lou Watson, early settler. Oral historical interview, Cleveland, Ohio, March 7, 1976.

[3] Gresham, op. cit.

[4] Arzell Gresham, oldest son of early settler. Oral historical interview, Cleveland, Ohio, December 29, 1985.

[5] Lovest Lee Watson, early settler. Oral historical interview, Cleveland, Ohio, March 4, 1976.

[6] Ibid.

[7] Ibid.

[8] Harvey Robinson, son of early settler. Oral historical interview, Cleveland, Ohio, December 29, 1985.

[9] Johnell Gresham, op. cit.

[10] Robinson, op. cit.

[11] Ibid.

[12] Wilbur H. Watson, *Aging and Social Behavior: An Introduction to Social Gerontology.* California: Wadsworth Health Sciences, **1982**.

[13] Lovest Lee Watson, early settler. Oral historical interview, Cleveland, Ohio, March 7, 1984.

[14]Wilbur H. Watson, *Older Poor Blacks and Social Services in the Rual Southern United States.* Washington, D.C.: The National Center on Black Aged, **1980**.

[15]Lovest Lee Watson, op. cit., June 25, 1984.

[16]Ibid.

[17]Ibid.

[18]C. A. Spencer, "Black Benevolent Societies and the Development of Black Insurance Companies in Nineteenth Century Alabama." *Phylon*, 46, 3 (September, 1985): 251-261.

[19]Ibid, p. 260.

[20]Lovest Lee Watson, op. cit., June 25, 1984.

Wade in the Water

[1]W.E.B. Dubois, *The Philadelphia Negro: A Social Study.* New York: Schocken Books, **1899**, p. 201.

[2]Eugene D. Genovese, *Roll Jordan Roll: The World the Slaves Made.* New York: Harper and Row, **1974**. Also see E. Franklin Frazier, *The Negro Church in America,* New York: Schocken Books, **1963**; also see Andrew Billingsley, *Black Families in White America,* Englewood Cliffs, New Jersey: Prentice Hall, Inc., **1968**.

[3]Lovest Lee Watson, early settler. Oral historical interview, December 26, 1983. These observations were corroborated by Sallie Mae Oatman, early settler, oral historical interview December 26, 1983.

[4]Nash Thompson, Jr., The History of the Canaan Missionary Baptist Church (Unpublished manuscript), Office of the Clerk, Canaan Missionary Baptist Church, 1969. The Canaan Missionary Baptist Church, now located at 4688 East 162nd Street (where it moved in 1981) was formerly located at 14701 Ohio Avenue, Cleveland, Ohio. This document, written by Nash Thompson, Jr., was made available by Mrs. Addie Crosby, an early resident of THE VILLAGE.

[5]John C. Ferguson, History of Saint Paul Methodist Church, Cleveland, Ohio, 1953. (Unpublished manuscript provided by Mrs. Mildred Hall, Church Historian and resident of THE VILLAGE, December, 1983.)

[6]Thompson, op. cit., p. 1. The full name of Reverend Jordan was not given in the "Historicy of Canaan," by Thompson nor in other sources available to this study.

[7]Ibid., p. 2.

[8]Ibid.

[9]Ibid., p. 3.

[10]Mary Robinson (Lewis) early settler. Oral historical interview by telephone, March 8, 1985. The full name of the Reverend Murray was unknown.

[11] John Slaughter, early settler. Oral historical interview by telephone, March 8, 1984.

[12] Thompson, op. cit., p. 4.

[13] Ibid., p. 3.

[14] Ibid.

[15] Ferguson, op. cit.

[16] Ibid., p. 3.

[17] Ibid., p. 3.

[18] Ibid., p. 4.

[19] Lovest Lee Watson, early settler, oral historical interview, March 3, 1984.

[20] Ferguson, op. cit., p. 4.

[21] Ibid.

[22] Ibid. Unfortunately, no details were given by Ferguson nor other sources on the exact location, for example building address, nor the specific date of the relocation of the Saint Paul group from the home of Edna Lee to the site on Lawndale Avenue.

[23] Ibid., p. 4-5.

[24] Ibid., p. 8.

[25] Ibid., p. 9.

[26] Ibid., p. 9.

[27] James Gary, Jr., son of early settler. Oral historical interview, April, 1974. Also Mary Lou Watson, early settler, oral historical interview, March 7, 1976.

[28] Sallie May Oatman, early settler. Oral historical interview, Monday, December 26, 1983.

[29] Ibid.

[30] Lovest Lee Watson, early settler. Oral historical interview, Sunday, December 25, 1983.

[31] John Slaughter, telephone interview, Thursday, March 8, 1984 in Cleveland, Ohio. Mr. Slaughter is a member of the New Home Baptist Church and husband of the former clerk of the church who is now deceased.

[32] Mrs. Jennie Noyes, telephone interview, March 8, 1984 in Cleveland, Ohio. Mrs. Noyes was, at the time of the interview, the records librarian of the American Baptist Churches of the United States of America, Cleveland, Ohio. The New Home Baptist Church is located at 15225 Sunview Avenue, in THE VILLAGE.

[33] The Reverend J. D. Smith, Assistant Pastor, Canaan Missionary Baptist Church. Oral historical interview, June 24, 1984.

[34] Donald G. Mathews *Religion in The Old South*. Chicago: The University of Chicago Press, **1977**, pp. 13, 24, 70.

[35] Ibid, pp. xvi-xvii.

[36] Lovest Lee Watson, early settler. Oral historical interview, December 26, 1983. The contents of this interview were corroborated by Sallie Mae Oatman, early settler, oral historical interview, December 26, 1983.

[37] Ibid.

[38] Marjorie Christine Watson, early settler. Letter written to Wilbur H. Watson, April 16, 1984.

[39] Mathews, op. cit., p. 71.

[40] W.E. B. Dubois, ed. *The Negro Church; Report of a Social Study,* Atlanta, GA: The Atlanta University Press, **1903**, p. 57.

[41] Ferguson, History of Saint Paul, Appendix.

[42] Frazier, *The Negro Church in America*, p. 44.

[43] Ibid.

[44] Carter G. Woodson, *The History of the Negro Church*, Washington, DC: The Associated Publishers, 1985, pp. 243-244.

[45] Arthur Huff Fausett, *Black Gods of the Metropolis: Negro Religious Cults in the Urban North*, Philadelphia, Pennsylvania: University of Pennsylvania Press, **1971**.

[46] Ibid.

[47] Ibid., p. 88.

[48] Ibid, p. 95.

[49] Arzel Gresham, oldest son of an early settler. Oral historical interview, Cleveland, Ohio, December 29, 1985.

[50] Woodson, op. cit., pp. 258-259.

[51] Frazier, op. cit.

[52] Woodson, op. cit., p. 255

[53] Ibid., pp. 255-256. Also see Alphonso Pinkney, *Black Americans*. Englewood Cliffs, New Jersey: Prentice-Hall, Inc., **1969**, p. 116.

[54] Pinkney, op. cit., p. 116.

[55] Woodson, op. cit., p. 256.

[56] Pinkney, op. cit., pp. 109-110.

⁵⁷Woodson, op. cit., pp. 244-246.

⁵⁸Ibid., p. 269.

⁵⁹See Genovese. op. cit.

Private Enterprise

¹W.E.B. Dubois, *The Black North in 1901,* New York: Arno Press and the New York Times, **1969.**

²Max Weber, *The Protestant Ethnic and the Spirit of Capitalism,* New York: Charles Scribner's Sons, **1958**, p. 172.

³Marge Banks, "She Recalls the Old Days in Miles Heights," *The Cleveland Press; Community News,* Thursday, December 4, **1969,** p. G-1.

⁴Martha Oatman, oral historical interview in her VILLAGE store, Friday, March 9, 1984.

⁵Ibid.

⁶Ibid.

⁷Crandell Gresham, current resident of THE VILLAGE, oral historical interview, June 27, 1984.

⁸Sandord Watson, oral historical interview, Cleveland, Ohio, June 26, 1984.

⁹Gresham, op. cit.

[10]Oatman, op. cit.

[11]Franklin Oatman, Oral historical interview, at his business office in THE VILLAGE, June 27, 1984.

[12]Lovest Lee Watson.

[13]Gresham, op. cit.

[14]John ZieMinski, telephone interview. Regional (Mass) Transit Authority, Cleveland, Ohio, June 27, 1984.

[15]Donald Sabath, "Lee-Seville Housing Battle Lines Drawn," *Cleveland Plain Dealer*, Friday, January 31, 1969, p. 10.

[16]Martha Oatman, op. cit.

[17]Gresham, op. cit.

[18]Addie Crosby-Jackson, oral historical interview in her home in THE VILLAGE, Tuesday, March 6, 1984.

[19]Martha Oatman, op. cit.; confirmed by oral historical interviews with Hobart Murray and Lovest Lee Watson, in THE VILLAGE, June 25, 1984.

[20]Lovest Lee Watson, oral historical interviews at his home in Cleveland, Ohio, December 23, 1983 and March 7, 1984.

[21]Ibid.

[22] Martha Oatman, op. cit.

[23] Marjorie C. Watson, oral historical interview at her home in Cleveland, Ohio, March 6, 1984.

[24] Martha Oatman, op. cit.

[25] Oliver Elie, Jr., oral historical interview by phone and in the family store, March 8, 1984.

[26] Gresham, op. cit.

[27] Ibid.

[28] Ibid.

[29] Hobart Murray, oral historical interview in THE VILLAGE, June 25, 1984.

[30] Ibid.

Summary and Conclusions

[1] William Ganson Rose, *Cleveland: The Making of a City*, Cleveland, OH: The World Publishing Co., **1950**, p. 1018.

[2] Ibid., p. 1044.

[3] Ibid.

[4] Op cit.

[5] John Sievenski, staff member of the Office of Services and Grant Development, Regional Transportation Authority, Cleveland, Ohio, telephone interview, June 25, 1984.

Afterword

[1] Alfred Schutz, "The World of Predecessors and the Problem of History." In Alfred Schutz, *Collected Papers, II: Studies in Social Theory* (Edited and Introduced by Arvid Brodersen), p. 8. The Hague, Netherlands: Martinus Nijhoff, **1964**,.

[2] George Herbert Mead, "History and the Experimental Method," In Anselm Strauss, Ed., *George Herbert Mead: On Social Psychology,* pp. 319-327, Chicago: University of Chicago Press, **1965**.

[3] David Dorsey, Professor of English, Atlanta University. Comments on an early draft of this chapter, September 28, 1984.

[4] Wilbur H. Watson and Robert J. Maxwell. *Human Aging and Dying: A Study in Sociocultural Gerontology,* New York: St. Martins Press, **1977**.

[5] L. L. Langness, *The Life History in Anthropological Science,* New York: Holt, Rinehart and Winston, **1965**.

[6] Herman Feifel, *Meanings of Death and Dying,* New York: Basic Books, **1978**; also see Mead, op. cit., p. 321.

⁷Robert S. Broadhead and Ray C. Rist, "Gatekeepers and the Social Control of Research," *Social Problems,* 23, 3 (February, **1976**): 325-336.

⁸Rhett S. Jones, "The Sociology of Knowledge: Proving Blacks Inferior, 1870-1930," *Black World,* 20, 4 (February, **1971**): 4-19.

⁹Wilbur H. Watson, "The Idea of Black Sociology: Its Cultural and Political Significance," *The American Sociologist,* 11 (May, **1976**): 115-123; Edwin M. Lemert, *Social Pathology,* New York: McGraw-Hill, **1951**; Joyce A. Ladner, ed. *The Death of White Sociology,* New York: Random House, **1973**, see especially Part III on "Black Sociology: Toward A Definition of Theory," pp. 167-252.

¹⁰Anne Mackay-Smith, "Paucity of Black Grad Students Keeps Faculties Lily White," *Perspective: The Atlanta Journal/Constitution,* Sunday, July 29, 1984, 5D, 7D.

¹¹Dwight W. Hoover, "Black History," In Martin Ballard, ed. *New Movements in the Study and Teaching of History,* p. 48. Bloomington and London: Indiana University Press, 1970; for another point of view on this issue see Ronald W. Walters, "Toward A Redefinition of Black Social Science," pp. 190-212 In Joyce Y. Ladner, ed. *The Death of White Sociology,* New York: Random House, **1973**.

¹²John Langston Gwalthney, *DryLongso: A Self-Portrait of Black America,* New York: Random House, **1981**.

[13] Barbara G. Meyerhoff and A. Simic', eds. *Life's Careers-Aging: Cultural Variations in Growing Old*, Beverly Hills, California: Sage, **1978**.

[14] Theodore R. Kennedy, *You Gotta Deal With It: Black Family Relations in a Southern Community*, New York: Oxford University Press, **1980**.

[15] Shutz, op. cit., pp. 52-68.

[16] Ibid, pp. 58-59.

[17] Ibid., p. 55.

[18] Ibid, p. 55-56.

[19] Wilbur H. Watson *A Multi-Method Approach to the Study of Older Blacks in the Rural South* (unpublished), Atlanta, Georgia: Department of Sociology, Atlanta University, 1980. Also see Langness, op. cit.; and John Dollard, *Class and Caste in a Southern Town*, New York: Doubleday, **1934**.

[20] Anthony Seldon and Joanna Pappworth, *By Word of Mouth: 'Elite' Oral History*, New York: Methuen, **1983**.

[21] National Union Catalog of Manuscript Collections, Information Circular No. 7, Library of Congress, Descriptive Cataloging Division, Manuscript Section, May, 1971.

[22] 'Oral History,' *Encyclopedia of Library and Information science*, 20 (New York, **1977**): 440.

[23] Seldon and Pappworth, op. cit., p. 4.

[24] National Union, op. cit.

[25] 'Oral History,' op. cit., p. 440.

[26] Morris Zelditch, Jr., "Some Methodological Problems of Field Studies," *American Journal of Sociology,* 67 **1962**: 566-576.

[27] Lee J. Cronbach, *Essentials of Psychological Testing,* New York: Harper and Brothers, **1960**.

[28] Robert N. Butler, "The Life Review: An Interpretation of Reminiscence in the Aged," In Bernice L. Neugarten, ed. *Middled Age and Aging: A Reader in Social Psychology*, pp. 486-496. Chicago: The University of Chicago Press, **1968**.

[29] Raymond B. Cattell, "The Structure of Intelligence in Relation to the Natural-Nurture Controversy," In Robert Cancro, ed. *Intelligence: Genetic and Environmental Influences,* pp. 3-30. New York: Grune and Stratton, **1971**.

[30] Watson, op. cit., **1980**.

[31] Dollard, op. cit.

[32] See, for example, Meyerhoff and Simic', op. cit., also see Carlos Castaneda, *The Eagle's Gift,* New York: Pocket Books, **1981**.

[33] Weber, op. cit.

[34] Wilbert E. Moore and Melvin M. Tumin, "Some Social Functions of Ignorance," *American Sociological Review*, 14, 5 (December, **1949**): 787-795; also see W.E.B. Dubois, "The Training of Negroes for Social Power," In the *Colored American Magazine,* May **1904,** pp. 333-339 reprinted in Philip S. Foner, ed., *W.E.B. Dubois Speaks: Speeches and Addresses,* Vol. 1 New York: Pathfinder, **1970.**

REFERENCES

Banks, Marge. "She Recalls the Old Days in Miles Heights." *The Cleveland Press Community News*. Thursday, December 4, 1969, p. G-1.

Barnett, Ida-Wells. *On Lynchings*. New York: Arno Press and the New York Times, **1969**.

Barr, Alwyn. *Black Texas: History of Negroes in Texas, 1528 - 1971*. Austin, Texas: Jenkins Publishing Company, **1973**.

Berger, Peter L. and Thomas Luckman. *The Social Construction of Reality: A Treatise in the Sociology of Knowledge*. New York: Anchor Books, **1966**.

Billingsley, Andrew. *The Black Family in White America*. Englewood Cliffs, New Jersey: Prentice-Hall, Inc., **1968**.

Blackwell, James E. *The Black Community: Diversity and Unity*, 2nd. Ed. New York: Harper and Row, **1985**.

Blauner, Robert. "Internal Colonailism and Ghetto Revolt." *Social Problems*. 16 (Spring **1969**): 393-408.

Broadhead, Robert S. and Ray C. Rist. "Gatekeepers and the Social Control of Research." *Social Problems*. 23, 3 (February 1976): 325-336.

Butler, Robert N. "The Life Review: An Interpretation of Reminiscence in the Aged." In Bernice L. Neugarten, Ed.

Middle Age and Aging: A Reader in Social Psychology, pp. 486-496. Chicago: The University of Chicago Press, **1968**.

Call and Post, Cleveland. "Ex-Mayor of Miles Heights Buried." Saturday, May 4, 1957, p. 6-A.

Call and Post, Cleveland. "Governor Bricker Appoints Race Man to Tax Division. Thursday, October 12, 1939, p. 3.

Castaneda, Carlos. *The Eagles's Gift.* New York: Pocket Books, **1981**.

Cattell, Raymond B. "The Structure of Intelligence in Relation to the Nature-Nurture Controversy." Robert Cancro, Ed. *Intelligence: Genetic and Environmental Influences*, pp. 3-30. New York: Grune and Stratton, **1971**.

Cronback, Lee J. *Essentials of Psychological Testing.* New York: Harper and Brothers, **1960**.

Davis, Allison, Burleigh B. Gardner and Mary R. Gardner. *Deep South: A Social Anthropological Study of Caste and Class.* Chicago: The University of Chicago Press, **1941**.

Davis, Russell H. *Black Americans in Cleveland: George Peake, the First Black Settler to Carl Stokes, the First Black Mayor.* Washington, D.C.: Associated Publishers, **1972**.

Dollard, John. *Class and Caste in a Southern Town.* New York: Doubleday, **1934**.

Drake, St. Clair and Horace R. Cayton. *Black Metropolis: A Study of Negro Life in a Northern City.* New York: Harper and Row, **1962** Edition.

Dubois, W. E. B., Ed. *The Negro Church; Report of a Social Study.* Atlanta, Georgia, The Atlanta University Press, **1903**, p. 57.

Dubois, W. E. B. *The Philadelphia Negro: A Social Study.* New York: Schocken Books, **1899**, p. 201.

Dubois, W. E. B. The Study of the Negro Problem" (Speech delivered by Dubois before the American Academy of Political and Social Science, November 19, 1897). Reprinted in Julius Lester, Ed. *The Seventh Son, I: The Thoughts and Writings of W. E. B. Dubois.* New York: Random House, **1971**, p. 229.

Dubois, W. E. B. *The Black North in 1901.* New York: Arno Press and the New York Times, **1969**.

Dubois, W. E. B. "The Training of Negroes for Social Power." In the *Colored American Magazine* May 1904, pp. 333-339 reprinted in Philip S. foner, Ed. *W. E. B. Dubois Speaks: Speeches and Addresses.* Vol. 1, New York: Pathfinder, **1970**.

Durkheim, Emile. *The Division of Labor in Society.* New York, New York: Free Press of Glencoe, **1964**.

Fiefel, Herman. *Meanings of Death and Dying*. New York: Basic Books, **1978**.

Frazier, E. Franklin. *The Negro Church in America*. New York: Schocken Books, **1963**.

Gans, Herbert J. *The Urban Villagers*. New York: Free Press of Glencoe, **1965**.

Genovese, Eugene D. *Roll Jordan Roll: The World the Slaves Made*. New York: Harper and Row, **1974**.

Geertz, Clifford. *The Interpretation of Cultures*. New York: Basic Books, **1973**.

Goffman, Erving. *Frame Analysis: An Essay on the Organization of Experience*. New York: Harper and Row, **1974**.

Greater Cleveland: A Bulletin on Public business by the Citizens League, Vol. V, No. 28 (April 10, 1930): 139-144.

Gwalthney, John Langston. *DryLongso: A Self-Portrait of Black America*. New York, Random House, **1981**.

Haekel, Josef. "Source Criticism in Anthropology." In Raoul Naroll and Ronald Cohen, Eds. *A Handbook of Method in Cultural Anthropology*, pp. 147-164. Garden City, New York: The Natural History Press, **1970**.

Horowitz, Irving Louis. "The Sociology Textbook: The Treatment of Conflict in American Sociological Literature." *International Social Science Council Information*. 11, 1 (February-August, 1972): 51-63.

Horowitz, Irving Louis. "The Sociology Textbook: The Treatment of Conflict in American Sociological Literature." *International Social Science Council Information*. 11, 1 (February-August, 1972): 51-63.

Hoover, Dwight W. "Black History." In Martin Ballard, Ed. *New Movements in the Study and Teaching of History*, pp. 32-49. Bloomington and London: Indiana University Press, **1970**.

Hughes, Langston and Arna Bontemps, Eds. *The Book of Negro Folklore*. New York: Dodd, Mead and Company, **1983**.

Hurston, Zora Neale. *Tell My Horse*. Turtle Island, South Carolina: Turtle Island Foundation, **1983**.

Ingram, Bill. "Miles Heights Was Really a Wild Town." Cleveland Press, April 4, **1969**, p. B-12.

James, William. "The Perception of Reality." In *Principles of Psychology*. Vol. 2, pp. 283-324. New York: Dover Publications, **1950**.

Jones, LeRoi. *Blues People*. New York: William Morrow and Company, **1963**.

Jones, Rhett S. "The Sociology of Knowledge: Proving Blacks Inferior, 1870-1930." *Black World*, 20, 4(February, 1971): 4-19.

Kuhn, Thomas S. *The Structure of Scientific Revolutions*. 2nd Ed. Chicago: University of Chicago Press, **1970**.

Ladner, Joyce A. Ed. *The Death of White Sociology*. New York: Random House, **1973**.

Langness, L. L. *The Life History in Anthropological Science*. New York: Holt, Rinehart and Winston, **1965**.

Lemert, Edwin M. *Social Pathology*. New York: McGraw-Hill, **1951**.

Lynd, Robert S. and Helen M. Lynd. *Middletown: A Study in American Culture*. New York: Harcourt, Brace, **1929**.

Mackay-Smith, Anne. "Paucity of Black Grad Students Keeps Faculties Lily White." *Perspective: The Atlanta Journal/Constitution*. Sunday, July 29, **1984**; 5-D, 7-D.

Mannheim, Karl. *Ideology and Utopia*. New York: Harcourt, Brace, adn World, Inc., **1936**.

Mathews, Donald G. *Religion in the Old South*. Chicago: The University of Chicago Press, **1977**.

Mead, George Herbert. "History and the Experimental Method." In Anselm Strauss, Ed. *George Herbert Mead: On Social Psychology*, pp. 319-327. Chicago: University of Chicago Press, **1964**.

Mead, George Herbert. "Time." In Anselm Strauss, Ed. *George Herbert Mead: On Social Psychology*, pp. 328-341. Chicago: University of Chicago Press, **1964**.

Merton, Robert K. "Notes on Problem-Finding in Sociology." In Robert K. Merton, Leonard Broom and Leonard S. Cottrell, Jr. *Sociology Today*, Vol. I: *Problems and Prospects*, pp. ix-xxxiv. New York: Harper Torchbooks, **1959**.

Meyerhoff, Barbara G. and A. Simic', Eds. *Life's Careers-Aging: Cultural Variations in Growing Old*. Beverly Hills, California: Sage, **1978**.

Moore, Wilbert E. and Melvin M. Tumin, "Some Social Functions of Ignorance." *American Sociological Review* 14, 5(December, **1949**): 787-795.

Myrdal, Gunnar. *Objectivity in Social Research*. New York: Pantheon Books, **1969**.

National Union Catalog of Manuscript Collections, Informatin Circular No. 7, Library of Congress, Descriptive Catloging Division, Manuscript Section, May, **1971**.

'Oral History.' *Encyclopedia of Library and Information Science*. 20 (New York, **1977**): 440.

Pinkeney, Alphonso. *Black Americans*. Englewood Cliffs, New Jersey: Prentice-Hall, Inc., **1969**.

Ploski, Harry A. and James Williams, Eds. *The Negro Almanac: A Reference Work on the Afro-American*. 4th Ed., p. 404. New York: John Wiley and Sons, **1983**.

Plain Dealer, Cleveland. "A. R. Johnston, County's First Negro Mayor is Dead at 65." Thursday, April 25, 1957, p. 13.

Plain Dealer, Cleveland. "Miles Heights is Annexed by City." March 29, 1932, p. 6.

Plain Dealer, Cleveland. "Miles Sanitation Imperils Health." April 27, 1932, p. 2.

Plain Dealer, Cleveland. "Miles Heights, Board Deadlocked; Schools Will Not Be Opened." October 2, 1931, p. 17.

Plain Dealer, Cleveland. "Schools Get Hope at Miles Heights." September 23, 1931, p. 4.

Polsby, Nelson W. *Community Power and Political Theory.* New Haven: Yale University Press, **1980**.

Press, The Cleveland. "Fight to Open Miles Heights School October 5." September 25, 1931, p. 16.

Press, The Cleveland. "She Recalls the Old Days in Miles Heights." *Community News*, Thursday, December 4, 1969, p. G-1.

Rose, William Ganson. *Cleveland: The Making of A City.* Cleveland: The World Publishing Company, **1950**, p. 1018.

Sabbath, Donald. "Lee-Seville Housing Battle Lines Drawn." *Cleveland Plain Dealer.* Friday, January 31, **1969**, p. 10.

Seldon, Anthony and Joanna Pappworth. *By Word of Mouth: 'Elite' Oral History.* New York: Methuen, **1983**.

Schuman, Howard, Charlotte Steeh and Lawrence Bobo. *Racial Attitudes In America: Trends and Interpretations*. Cambridge, Massachusetts: Harvard Universtiy Press, **1985**.

Schutz, Alfred, "The World of Predecessors and the Problem of History." In Alfred Schutz, *Collected Papers, II: Studies in Social Theory*, pp. 56-63. (Edited and Introduced by Arvid Brodersen). The Hague, Netherlands: Martinus Nijhoff, **1964**.

Spencer, C. A. "Black Benevolent Societies and the Development of Black Insurance Companies in Nineteenth Century Alabama." *Phylon*, 46, 3 (September, 1985): 251-261.

Suttles, Gerald D. *The Social Order of the Slum: Ethnicity and Territory* in the Inner city. Chicago: Unviersity of Chicago Press, **1968**.

Tonnies, Ferdinand. *Community and Society: Gemeinschaft and Gesselschaft*. Charles P. Loomis, ed. East Lansing, Michigan: Michigan State University Press, **1957**.

Vidich, Arthur J. and Joseph Bensman. *Small Town in Mass Society: Class, Power, and Religion in a Rural Society*. New York: Anchor Books, **1960**.

Walters, Ronald W. "Toward a Redefinition of Black Social Science." In Joyce Y. Ladner, ed. *The Death of White Sociology*, pp. 190-212. New York: Random House, 1973.

Watson, Sharon M. "The Second Time Around: A Profile of Black Mayoral Reelection Campaigns." *Phylon* 45, 3 (September, 1984): 165-178.

Watson, Wilbur H. *Aging and Social Behavior: An Introduction to Social Gerontology.* California: Wadsworth Health Science, **1982**.

Watson, Wilbur H. and Robert J. Maxwell. *Human Aging and Dying: A Study in Sociocultural Gerontology.* New York: St. Martins Press, **1977**.

Watson, Wilbur H. *Older Poor Blacks and Social Services in the Rural Southern United States.* Washington, D.C.: The National Center on Black Aged, **1980**.

Watson, Wilbur H. "The Idea of Black Sociology: Its Cultural and Political Significance." *The American Sociologist* 11, 2 (May, 1976): 115-123.

Watson, Wilbur H. "A Multi-Method Approach to the Study of Older Blacks in the Rural South." (Atlanta, Georgia: Department of Sociology, Atlanta University, **1980** (unpublished).

Weber, Max. *The Methodology of the Social Sciences* (Translated and Edited by E. A. Shils and H. A. Finch). New York: The Free Press, **1949**.

Weber, Max. *The Protestant Ethnic and the Spirit of Capitalism.* New York: Charles Scribner's Sons, **1958**, p. 172.

Whiting, Beatrice and John Whiting. "Methods for Observing and Recording Behavior." In Raoul Naroll and Ronald Cohen, Eds. *A Handbook of Method in Cultural Anthropology*, pp. 282-315. Garden City, New York: The Natural History Press, **1970**.

Wirth, Luis. *The Ghetto*. Chicago: The University of Chicago Press, **1956.**

Woodson, Carter G. *The History of the Negro Church*. Washington, D.C.: The Associated Publishers, **1985.**

Subject Index

Annexation, 24, 62-63.

  Black Registered Voters and, 63.
  Sewage Services and, 70.

Atlanta Life Insurance Company, 78.

Begging for the Deceased Poor, 76-77.

Beehive School, 58-61, 125-126.

"Belle Villa," 15.

Bereavement, 75-77.

Black Republicans, 51-52.

  Block Voting, 51.
  Registered Voters, 62.

Business, Small, 106-123.

  Churches and, 98-100, 111.
  Early Development, 107.
  Economic Depression and, 108.
  Family owned, 14.
  Population Growth and, 110.
  Rise of Utility Companies and, 115-116.

Canaan Missionary Baptist Church, 81-84.

Church, xiii.

  Africans and, 80.
  Baptists, 81-84, 92-94.
  Catholics, 81, 85.
  Concept of Family Church, 96-97.
  Methodists, 81, 84-92.
  Social Functions of, xiii, 94-104.

Community, Concept of, viii.

  Paradigms of, vii-viii.
  Sense of, xi-xiii.

Doctor, Country, 70, 72.

  Transportation Problems, 72-73.

Death, 75-76.

Burial for the Poor, 76.

Depression of 1930s, 23, 56-57, 76, 106-108, 110, 127-128.

  Prizefighting and, 39-40.

Ethnic Diversity, 15-19.

  Southern Origins, 16.

Ethnocentrism, 137-138.

Explanation, Historical, 7.

Fact, Nature of, 8.

  Theory and 7.

Family Church, Concept of, 96-97.

Folk hero, 32-43.

  Definition of, 32.
  Pugilist as, 38.

Gemeinschaft, vii.

Gesellschaft, vii.

Golden Gloves, 38.

Brooks family, 41.

Hawker, xiii-xiv.

Health, 61-62.

  Country Doctors and, 70.
  Midwives and, 66, 70-75.
  Survey of 1932, 61.

Hero, 32

  Pugilist, 34.

Historiography, 5-6.

  Limitations of, 134-137.
  Ethnocentrism and, 137-140.

History, 133.

"Honey Dipper," 68.

Hospitals, 66-67, 72.

Housing construction, 14, 117-118.

Insiders, 37, 52.

Insurance, Burial and Life, 77-79.

Early Black Companies, 78.

Johnston, Arthur R., xv-xvi, 2, 126-127.

   Amateur pugilist, 42.
   Church Memberships, 48-49.
   Cleveland Director of Purchases, 64.
   Commitment to Service, 48.
   Electoral Victories, 45.
   Mayor of old Miles Heights, 44-46, 49-55.
   Medical Education, 46.
   Military Service, 47.
   Naturalization as Citizen of U.S., 47.
   Tax Examiner, 64.

Jordan, Twentieth Century, 4.

Line Settlement, 19.

Marriages, Interracial, xi, 19-23.

   Chidlren of, 23.

Mass Transporation, 117, 129.

Mechanical solidariy, vii.

Memory Retention in Oral Historical Research, 143-147.

   Alzheimer's Disease and, 147.
   Apoplexy and, 146.
   Blindness and, 147.
   Chronic Brain Syndrome and, 146.
   Hearing Impairment and, 147.
   In Relation To In-depth Interviews, 146.

Midwives, 66, 70-75.

Miles Heights Reunion, 28-31.

Oatman's Store, 14.

Oral History, 140-148.

   Cross-Validating Results, 144.
   Defined, 143.
   Limitations of, 151-152.
   Lived Experience, 143-144.

Organic Solidarity, vii.

Outhouses, 67-69.

   Defined, 68.

"Honey Dipper," 68.

Outsiders, 52.

Police as, 34.
Insiders and, 37, 52.

Peddler, 111-112.

Peer Groups, 25.

The "Nucleus," 25-27.

Picnics, 28.

Politics, 44-65.

Poverty, 77-79.

Prizefighting:

As Escape From Poverty, xi.

Protestant Ethnic, 107.

Pugilist, 38.

A. R. Johnston as, 42.
Nate Brooks as, 38-42.

"Race Man," 3.

Racial Attitudes, 22.

Segregation and, 35.
Sports and, 41.

Reality, Social Construction of, ix.

Reciprocity, Ethnic of, xi.

Registered Black Voters, 62-63.

Reunions:

Family, xi.
Picnics, xii, 28.
Social Clubs, xi, 27-29.

Roles, vii.

Sanitation, 67-75.

School, xiii.

Beehive, 58-61.
Church Teaching, 102-104.

Self Help, x, 73, 70.

Midwifery, 73-75.
Poor and Bereaved, 75-77.

Settlers, Early, 13, 81.

  Whites, 81.

Seville Homes, 117-118, 128-129.

Social History:
Definition of, 6-7.
Social construction of, xiv, 6.

Social Bonds, xi-xii.

  Peer Groups, 25.
  Nucleus, 27-29.

Stokes, Carl R., ix, xv-xvi.

Story Telling, xviii-xix.

  Analysis of, xix.

St. Paul's Methodist Church, 84-92.

They-relations, 1, 141.

Time; Mead's Concept of, 9.

Togetherness, 76.

Transporation, Public, 73.

  Cleveland, 117, 129.

Vendors, 111-117.

  Agressive, 112.
  Hawker, xiii-xiv, 112-115.
  Passive, 112-114.

Voter Complacency, 51.

We-relations, 1, 133, 140-142.

White Residents, 85, 107.

World War II, 24.